W9-ACL-364

WITHDRAWN
L. R. COLLEGE LIBRARY

CARL A. RUDISILL LIBRARY
LENOIR-RHYNE COLLEGE

BREAKING LEGS

BREAKING LEGS

by

Tom Dulack

Garden City, New York

CARL A. RUDISILL LIBRARY
LENOIR-RHYNE COLLEGE

Copyright © 1992 by Tom Dulack

PS
3554
.U4
B74
1992
oct.1998

CAUTION: Professionals and amateurs are hereby warned that BREAKING LEGS is subject to a royalty. It is fully protected under the copyright laws of the United States of America, and of all countries covered by the International Copyright Union (including the Dominion of Canada and the rest of the British Commonwealth), and of all countries covered by the Pan-American Copyright Convention and the Universal Copyright Convention, and of all countries with which the United States has reciprocal copyright relations. All rights, including professional, amateur, motion picture, recitation, lecturing, public reading, radio broadcasting, television, video or sound taping, all other forms of mechanical or electronic reproduction, such as information storage and retrieval systems and photocopying, and the rights of translation into foreign languages, are strictly reserved. Particular emphasis is laid upon the question of readings, permission for which must be secured from the author's agent in writing.

The stage performance rights in BREAKING LEGS (other than first class rights) are controlled exclusively by the DRAMATISTS PLAY SERVICE, INC., 440 Park Avenue South, New York, N.Y. 10016. No professional or non-professional performance of the play (excluding first class professional performance) may be given without obtaining in advance the written permission of the DRAMATISTS PLAY SERVICE, INC., and paying the requisite fee.

Inquiries concerning all other rights should be addressed to Gilbert Parker, c/o William Morris Agency, Inc., 1350 Avenue of the Americas, New York, N.Y. 10019.

ISBN: 1-56865-035-3

Photos of the cast of the national tour by Janet Van Ham
Book design by Maria Chiarino
Manufactured in the United States of America

BREAKING LEGS was produced by Elliot Martin, Bud Yorkin and James and Maureen O'Sullivan Cushing at the Promenade Theatre in New York City in May 1991. It was directed by John Tillinger, the set design was by James Noone, the costume design was by David C. Woolard, the lighting design was by Ken Billington and the production stage manager was Elliott Woodruff. The cast was as follows:

LOU GRAZIANO . . . . Vincent Gardenia
ANGIE GRAZIANO . . . . Sue Giosa
TERENCE O'KEEFE . . . . Nicolas Surovy
MIKE FRANCISCO . . . . Philip Bosco
TINO DE FELICE . . . . Victor Argo
FRANKIE SALVUCCI . . . . Larry Storch

BREAKING LEGS was produced by the Berkshire Theatre Festival (Richard Dunlap, Artistic Director; Chuck Still, Managing Director) in Stockbridge, Massachusetts, on July 17, 1990. It was directed by John Tillinger, the set design was by James Noone, the costume design was by David C. Woolard, the lighting design was by Arden Fingerhut, the sound design was by Scott David Sanders and the stage manager was C.A. Clark. The cast was as follows:

LOU GRAZIANO . . . . Dick Latessa
ANGIE GRAZIANO . . . . Sue Giosa
TERENCE O'KEEFE . . . . John McMartin
MIKE FRANCISCO . . . . Raymond Serra
TINO DE FELICE . . . . Lou Tiano
FRANKIE SALVUCCI . . . . Eddie Zammit

BREAKING LEGS received its world premiere at the Old Globe Theatre (Jack O'Brien, Artistic Director; Thomas Hall, Managing Director) in San Diego, California, on September 6, 1989. It was directed by Jack O'Brien, the set design was by Cliff Faulkner, the custome design was by Robert Wojewodski, the lighting design was by John B. Forbes, the sound design was by Jeff Ladman and the stage manager was Hollie Hopson. The cast was as follows:

LOU GRAZIANO . . . . T.J. Castronovo
ANGIE GRAZIANO . . . . Sue Giosa
TERENCE O'KEEFE . . . . Greg Mullavey
MIKE FRANCISCO . . . . Mike Genovese
TINO DE FELICE . . . . Richard Kneeland
FRANKIE SALVUCCI . . . . Eddie Zammit

CAST OF CHARACTERS

TERENCE O'KEEFE, in his late 40s, early 50s, a playwright, English professor
LOU GRAZIANO, 55, the proprietor of a restaurant
ANGIE, 28, his daughter
MIKE FRANCISCO, in his late 50s, a man who is sometimes mistaken for a mobster
TINO DE FELICE, in his 50s, a businessman
FRANKIE SALVUCCI, in his 50s, a horse-player

TIME

The Present

PLACE

A restaurant in a New England university town

This play is for all my Belgian brothers and sisters:
Hen and Françoise, Paul and Piloute,
Anne and Livio, Didi and ZaZa.

Act I

ACT I

*The back room of an Italian restaurant in New England.
It's a private room used for parties; there's a semi-
circular booth stage right; a service bar with a couple of
stools upstage left; and in front of that a table, checkered
tablecloth, candle in a Chianti bottle, three chairs. Plastic
flowers and ferns, fountains and garden sculpture com-
prise the interior decorating scheme.*

*Upstage is a door leading to the main dining room, and
stage left, at the side of the bar, is another door leading
to the kitchen. Stage right, behind the booth, a large window overlooks an alley adjacent to the parking lot.*

In the restaurant. LOU *and* ANGIE, *a flamboyant rather
tough young woman in a miniskirt and high heels.*

LOU: So what happened?

ANGIE *(opening mail):* Nothing happened. What is this,
469 dollars from Semprini Plumbing?

LOU: They fixed the toilets in the women's john. So what
did he do?

ANGIE: Nothing! Forget it! I thought Semprini owed you
a favor.

LOU: He did.

ANGIE: 469 dollars? This is a favor? What's he got to do, stick a coat hanger down there, for the love of God.

LOU: Hey, what do I know? His work is guaranteed.

ANGIE: It better be guaranteed!

LOU: Lay off Charlie, he's a nice guy.

ANGIE: Nice, nice.

LOU: You know, it's none of my business, Angel, but you date a guy for fifteen months, what are we supposed to think?

ANGIE: Why do you have to think anything?

LOU: What, I'm not human? Your daughter dates some guy for a year and a half, I'm not supposed to *think?*

ANGIE: He's a creep.

LOU: It took you a year and a half to figure out he's a creep?

ANGIE: I was giving him the benefit of the doubt. (*Opening an envelope and reading.*) Mosconi's got a good price on calamar'.

LOU: We can't buy no fish products from Mosconi. I told you before. My father would turn over in his grave.

ANGIE: Giuliani gave us some fish we had complaints last week.

LOU: He had an accident with his refrigerator.

ANGIE: It's not the first time either.

LOU: You know, your grandmother liked this guy.

ANGIE: I don't want to talk about it.

LOU: All I'm saying is she's gonna take this hard. She was counting on you to give her some great-grandchildren before she dies.

ANGIE: She's already got about forty of them. How many does she need?

LOU: You can never have too many. And what about me?

ANGIE: What about you?

LOU: I ain't getting any younger. A man wants to see his daughter settle down, raise a family. I want to play with your kids, take 'em fishing, take 'em to the race track, teach 'em how to shoot craps.

ANGIE: You know, our payroll's too big. Why do we need Francine Saturday afternoons? We don't do dick Saturday afternoons.

LOU: Look, Angel, this is none of my business, and I don't want to interfere in your private life. But you know, I mean, you gotta start thinking about your future. Naturally you want to be selective, and a girl like you can afford to bide your time. Still, you're getting to the age—I mean, don't get me wrong, Angel, everybody thinks you're 22, 23, 26 . . . still—

ANGIE: Dad, Marvin is history, okay? Ancient history!

LOU: Yeah, well, I knew it would never work. From the beginning, I told your mother, "Don't get your hopes up. This creep just ain't got what it takes."

ANGIE: I'm gonna put Francine in the kitchen Saturday afternoons. What time's Terence coming?

LOU: I told him to come early. Mike's gotta go someplace tonight.

ANGIE: I can't wait to see him again. He was such a great teacher.

LOU: He said they did one of his plays in Europe.

ANGIE: Oh yeah?

LOU: Now he wants to do it in New York. He's looking for investors.

ANGIE: So what do you guys know about producing plays?

LOU: What's there to know? How hard can it be?

ANGIE: Everybody I ever heard of invested in a play they lost their shirt.

LOU: You lose your shirt at the track, shooting craps, what's the difference? It'll be nice, it'll be a laugh. Opening night, pulling up to the door in a stretch limousine. Red carpet on the sidewalks, Connie

Chung, Channel 5 News. Some bimbo on my arm. You're gonna lose your shirt, you might as well go in style.

ANGIE: Never mind the bimbo on your arm.

LOU: You don't have to repeat that to your mother. I was only kidding.

ANGIE: Well, when Terry comes, just remember who you're dealing with. Don't embarrass me.

LOU: "Embarrass you!" What's that suppose to mean? Since when do I embarrass you?

ANGIE: He's a college professor, that's all I'm saying.

LOU: What are you, telling me something I don't know? I don't know he's a college professor now?

ANGIE: All I'm saying is he's not some scumbag looking to put the bite on you, like Dino or Vinnie. You can't be jerking him around.

LOU: Nobody's gonna jerk him around! Whatsa matter with you?

ANGIE: Just remember who you're dealing with, that's all I'm saying. Did you eat yet?

LOU: Nah, I'll wait for Mike and Tino. Whata we got tonight.

ANGIE: I don't know, I'll go see.

LOU: And ask Billy who won the fifth at Hialeah. Patsy had a horse running down there. (ANGIE *goes out.*) And call your Aunt Mary! How many times I have to tell you?

ANGIE *(offstage):* Okay, okay!

TERENCE *(entering by the upstage door, calling):* Lou? Lou? Hello?

LOU: Hey, Professor! How ya doing? (TERENCE *is a good-looking, physically fit man in his late 40s or early 50s. He is not in any way the image of a bumbling absent-minded, ivory-tower English teacher. To his female students he is a stud, and an object of their sex fantasies. He is a world traveler, urbane, sophisticated. But he is an intellectual and he's shy, feels out of place here in* ANGIE's *restaurant, and awkward about his reason for being there—to ask for money. He is wearing a raincoat and carrying a briefcase. He and* LOU *shake hands enthusiastically.*)

TERENCE: Lou! Good to see you!

LOU: Believe me when I tell you, you're looking great!

TERENCE: Thanks, Lou. So are you.

LOU: Gimme your coat. Terrible weather.

TERENCE *(taking off his coat):* Yeah, there was a really bad accident on the turnpike just outside of Bridgeport.

LOU: Is that right?

TERENCE: It was raining so hard, this little sports car, I guess it was going too fast. Just got flattened by a semi. It was awful. Bodies all over the place.

LOU: Well, we're lucky it ain't snow. Don't laugh. It snowed October 6th last year, remember?

TERENCE: No, I was in Europe. Did you have snow?

LOU: You know what they say about the weather in New England. Who was that famous writer—you ought to know this—this writer, who the hell was he, who said, "If you don't like the weather in New England— tough shit!" Something like that. Who said that, Professor? Wendell Oliver Holmes?

TERENCE: Actually, you're thinking of Mark Twain, Lou, but what he really said was, "If you don't like the weather in New England—"

LOU: Yeah, yeah, whatever he said, forget it, sit down. So tell me the truth, Professor, how's it going?

TERENCE: Good, Lou, real good. Not bad at all. Can't really complain.

LOU: So, you got a new play.

TERENCE: Yeah, that's right, got a new play.

LOU: That's great. You hungry, Professor? How about a cocktail?

TERENCE: Oh, I don't know, yeah, you know, whatever.

LOU (*as he crosses to the bar to get glasses):* My partners be here any minute. So, what, you're looking to produce this play of yours Off-Broadway?

TERENCE: Off-off-Broadway.

LOU: Off-off? I didn't know there was Off-off.

TERENCE: Oh yeah. These days, they're even beginning to talk about Off-off-off. (LOU *is so impressed by this concept he forgets he's offered* TERENCE *a drink)*

LOU: Off-off-off! Is that right? This I didn't know, Professor.

TERENCE: Actually, in Off-off you tend to find plays with a lot more artistic integrity than you do off or God knows on. It's a question of the kind of play you have. *Cats,* something like that, *Phantom of the Opera,* they could only be on Broadway. Other plays do better elsewhere.

LOU: And you're convinced that Off-off is right for you.

TERENCE: Well, naturally, you always hope to move up. With good reviews. It's difficult to explain, Lou.

LOU: Yeah, well, anyway, opening night they still do the bit with stretch limousines, right, even Off-off?

TERENCE: Stretch limousines?

LOU: What I mean to say, searchlights in the sky, Connie Chung, like that?

TERENCE: Connie Chung? Oh, sure! Well, I mean. Well, sure. I'm sure Connie Chung goes to see plays Off-off Broadway. From time to time. Sure, Lou. I think I'll have that drink now.

LOU: Great! Whataya gonna have? Angie! Look who's here! Angie! Angie! (ANGIE *enters*)

ANGIE: Geez! Terence! It's so great to see you again! (TERENCE *embraces her chastely*)

TERENCE: It's great to see you too.

ANGIE: You look fantastic!

TERENCE: So do you.

ANGIE: Europe must of agreed with you. So where were you, exactly?

TERENCE: In Belgium most of the time.

ANGIE: Belgium! Wow! Where is that, in France?

TERENCE: Between France and Germany.

ANGIE: I was never strong in geography.

LOU: She don't have a scholarly temperament, Professor. Angie's not a student.

TERENCE: She could have been a wonderful student if she hadn't dropped out of school. Some of those short stories she wrote for me were the most original things I ever got from a student.

LOU: Yeah, well, she was pretty original with the books around here too. Three weeks running this joint she had the payroll so screwed up I had to rent a computer to get things straightened out.

ANGIE: That'll be the day my father puts the payroll on a computer! So what can I get you, Terence?

TERENCE: I don't know. A vodka, I guess. Yeah, bring me a vodka on the rocks. Vodka, twist of lemon.

LOU: What's the special today, hon?

ANGIE: Risotto Sicilian. That's rice with tomato sauce and pieces of fish.

LOU: Bring us a little side, just to taste, and maybe a plate of antipasto.

ANGIE: Do you want something to drink, Dad?

LOU: Nah, I don't feel like nothing right now, hon. And when Mike and Tino come, tell Francine send 'em back here. They're probably gonna eat. Maybe Joey too.

ANGIE: Oh yeah, I forgot to tell you, Frankie Salvucci called.

LOU: Frankie Salvucci? What'd he say?

ANGIE: He said he had to talk to you, it was urgent, he was coming around tonight.

LOU: Okay, doll.

ANGIE: Be right back. *(She goes out)*

LOU *(watching her go, fondly):* Hell of a kid.

TERENCE: Yeah, she is.

LOU: Knockout, huh? Tell me the truth. She's turned into a knockout.

TERENCE: She always was a knockout. You know, it's none of my business, Lou, but it's such a waste she doesn't get her degree.

LOU: What's she need with a degree? All due respect, Professor, how old are you? 42? 44? 46?

TERENCE: Around there.

LOU: And you got what? Three degrees? Four? You're a professor at the university. Whataya make? Forty grand? 42? 44?

TERENCE: Around forty grand.

LOU: And whataya drivin'? I bet you're driving some beat-up old Rabbit on its final legs—am I right or wrong? *(Not waiting for his reply)* No offense intended, Professor. But Angie's . . . 25, and she makes fifty grand working for me. She's driving a brand new Alfa Romeo and she owns two condos in Boca. Tell me the truth, what's that kid need with a degree?

TERENCE: Well, you put it like that. . . . You know. It's just that she had a gift.

LOU: So maybe one day she'll go back in her spare time. What? There some statue of limitations or whatever to get your degree?

TERENCE: Seven years, I think, after you quit. She dropped out, what, '79? '80?

LOU: Whatever it was, she decides to go back and finish I'm sure you can put in a word for her and fix things up.

TERENCE: Oh, sure, absolutely, I'd love to.

LOU: It's the same in the university like anywhere else, it's a question of who you know to get things done, right, Professor?

TERENCE: Right.

LOU: My point exactly. So how much money you need for this play of yours? You said on the phone a hundred grand?

TERENCE: Around there.

LOU: Don't sound like much.

TERENCE: It doesn't?

LOU: When you need the money, Terence? I mean to say, how soon?

TERENCE: Wait, you understand, I'm not asking for a loan. I've already raised $30,000.

LOU: I and my partners, we give you the money, how soon can you get under way? Like say we give you the money today.

TERENCE: You mean you might give me all of it? Jesus, I don't know. It never crossed my mind that. . . . Well, if you gave me the money today, we could start, I guess, tomorrow, signing the actors and . . .

LOU: Good, good, that's very good, Professor. I think my partners will find this a very interesting opportunity. (ANGIE *returns with a tray of antipasto, the side of fish and rice, and the cocktail*)

ANGIE: There you are.

LOU: And bring us some bread, hon, and some hot peppers. You like hot peppers on your fish and rice, Terence?

TERENCE: I don't know, I never tried it.

LOU: You'll love it. And bring us a side of primavera, doll. You like primavera?

TERENCE: I don't know.

ANGIE *(anticipating)*: You'll love it. It's chicken and vegetables with pasta in a white sauce.

LOU: It's terrific. And some bread, Angel. I asked you three times already for the bread.

ANGIE: Okay, okay!

LOU: And some hot peppers while you're at it! *(She goes)* Eat, Terence. Try the antipasto. How's your cocktail? Just the way you like it?

TERENCE: Yes, fine. Cheers. *(He manages to avoid eating. LOU doesn't notice—he is busy eating himself)*

LOU: So your other play went over big in Europe, is that right?

TERENCE: Very big. We had three productions. One in Belgium, one in Switzerland and one in Sweden.

LOU: That's wonderful. It must have been a wonderful experience. I'm happy for you.

TERENCE: Thanks.

LOU: How do you explain the fact that it flopped in New York?

TERENCE: I don't. Different cultures. I don't know. *(Enter ANGIE with hot peppers)*

ANGIE: Hot peppers.

TERENCE: Thank you.

ANGIE: The bread's in the oven.

LOU: Thanks, doll. Hey, I just saw Mike and Tino pull in. Go tell 'em we're back here. And tell Francine to put that party of six at the round table. What the hell's the matter with her? She must be drunk. Hurry up, will ya, honey?

ANGIE *(going off, irritably)*: Okay, okay!

LOU: Hell of a kid, huh, Professor? Make somebody a hell of a wife. *(He looks into the dining room)* God damn it! I told Francine a million times! Nobody does what you tell them, might as well save your breath! Excuse me a minute, Professor. Enjoy your cocktail. Try the antipasto. Relax. Make yourself at home. *(He goes out. Alone,* TERENCE *takes the script of his play out of his briefcase, along with some legal documents he wants to review before making his presentation to his potential investors.* ANGIE *returns with a basket of bread and the primavera)*

ANGIE: Here's your bread, where'd he go?

TERENCE: I don't know.

ANGIE *(with a sigh)*: Sometimes it's not easy working with your father.

TERENCE: Thanks. So, then you've made up your mind then that this is what you're going to do for the rest of your life?

ANGIE: I don't know. How's your drink?

TERENCE: Fine.

ANGIE: I don't know. It's interesting work, meeting the public. Every day is interesting. I could never work in an office nine to five. Try the primavera. It's nice, you'll love it.

TERENCE: Thanks. *(But for the moment he doesn't try it)*

ANGIE: And the pay is very good. My father says I'll be a rich woman by the time I'm forty.

TERENCE: Nothing wrong with that.

ANGIE: I know, but there's something missing. I feel like . . . I don't know . . . it's not what I dreamed about when I was a kid.

TERENCE: What *did* you dream about?

ANGIE: Oh, you know, the usual thing. Being famous. Being a movie star. Stupid, huh? *(She rinses and dries some cups and saucers. He sits on a bar stool)*

TERENCE: What's stupid?

ANGIE: Look at me: big nose, big ass.

TERENCE: Sophia Loren had a big . . . uh . . . nose.

ANGIE: Did you really think I had something in your class?

TERENCE: I still remember one of your stories about a young girl's first . . . her first . . . "awakening" to the sensual aspect of . . . to the confused, adolescent emotional realities of young love.

ANGIE: Oh yeah. That thing about the first time I did it. So, that turned you on, or what?

TERENCE: I thought it was full of power and . . . and originality. Some echo of a literary sensibility that reminded me of a young D.H. Lawrence, actually.

ANGIE: I never would of quit school if my other teachers were like you. But God, they were so boring! Chaucer and Milton, you know what I mean? *You* could of made me like Chaucer and Milton.

TERENCE: Well, nevertheless, I think you should have stayed and gotten your degree.

ANGIE: I thought life was passing me by. I got scared. Maybe if you would of been around to talk to—but you went on your sabbatical my sophomore year and I didn't have anybody to talk to. Funny thing is, now it still feels like life is passing me by.

TERENCE: You can always come back. I was telling your dad . . .

ANGIE: Nah, I'm too spoiled. Money, cars, pleasures of the flesh. So you've written a new play?

TERENCE: Yeah, I'm trying to interest your dad and his partners to invest some money.

ANGIE: I think that's a very good idea. They're loaded. They don't know what to do with it.

TERENCE: Well, that's interesting. But the play's very controversial.

ANGIE: Oh yeah?

TERENCE (*pompously*): Yes, it's the first time in the Modern Theatre that a play examines the question of murder the way I do.

ANGIE: What is it?

TERENCE: What is what?

ANGIE: What is the question? The question of murder.

TERENCE: Well, I mean, I'm trying to bring it home to the audience to make them *feel*, actually *feel* what it's like to kill someone. It's very strong stuff. Powerful. Sickening, actually. It takes a strong stomach. I hope your dad isn't scared off by it.

ANGIE: Oh, I don't think so. It sounds like quite a play.

TERENCE: It was a big hit last year in Buffalo.

ANGIE: They do plays in Buffalo?

TERENCE: Sure, they do a lot of plays in Buffalo.

ANGIE: Where people actually get paid and stuff?

TERENCE: Well, you don't get paid much.

ANGIE: It's funny, you just never think about Buffalo being a place where they do plays.

TERENCE: I guess it's funny. I never thought about it.

ANGIE: Me neither. So then have you ever killed anybody?

TERENCE: *Killed* anybody!

ANGIE: I mean personally. Have you ever *personally* killed anybody?

TERENCE: God no! What an idea!

ANGIE: But then how can you show this murder on stage? How can you make the people in the audience feel what it's like if you don't know?

TERENCE: What a naive question!

ANGIE: So in other words you just make it up about this murder.

TERENCE: Any author just makes it up. Shakespeare just made it up. Dostoyevsky. Conan Doyle.

ANGIE: Uh huh. Well, that sounds fascinating. So then about raising the money, you just went down mentally a list in your mind of all the rich people you knew? Or what?

TERENCE: All the rich and all the poor people I know. Family, friends, relatives. *(Finished with her cleaning up behind the service bar, she sits at the small table where she served the antipasto and the primavera. He joins her)*

ANGIE: Is it so hard to raise money?

TERENCE: It's terrible. It used to be you could try for a grant—the Rockefeller Foundation, the NEA. Not any more. I've been trying to finance this play for three years now.

ANGIE: Three years! Don't you get discouraged?

TERENCE: No, not really. You remember what Goethe said.

ANGIE *(after a pause):* No. What did he say?

TERENCE: "Life is short, but art is long." If you really believe in something, you don't get discouraged.

ANGIE: Sounds like this play is pretty important to you.

TERENCE: I guess when all is said and done, it's just about the most important thing in my life.

From left to right, Joseph Mascolo as Mike Francisco, Gary Sandy as Terence O'Keefe, Karen Valentine as Angie Graziano, Larry Storch as Frankie Salvucci, Vince Viverito as Tino De Felice and Vincent Gardenia as Lou Graziano.

All photos of the original cast of the 1992 national tour by Janet Van Ham.

Joseph Mascolo (left) as Mike with
Vincent Gardenia as Lou.

Vincent Gardenia (left) as Lou with Karen Valentine (center) as Angie and Gary Sandy (right) as Terence.

ANGIE: Well, you came to the right place then. These guys drop in one night shooting craps probably twice as much as you need for your play. (*Absently, he has picked up something fiery from the plate of antipasto and bites into it. He chokes, gulps at his drink*)

TERENCE: They do?

ANGIE: Oh, you got no idea.

TERENCE: Well, that's encouraging.

ANGIE: Believe me, you got nothing to worry about. Anyway, I'm really glad you decided to ask my Dad. It's really great to see you again.

TERENCE: You too.

ANGIE: I always wondered why you never asked me out.

TERENCE: What do you mean? How could I ask you out? When?

ANGIE: In school, when I was in your class. I always thought you were interested. It looked like you were looking.

TERENCE: Well, naturally I looked. You're hard not to look at.

ANGIE: But I guess that's all it was, huh? You were *just* looking. You weren't really interested.

TERENCE: In fact, I have to confess, belatedly, I *was* really interested.

ANGIE: I'm never wrong about these things. So then why didn't you ask me out?

TERENCE: Because I was too old for you, and besides that, of course—

ANGIE: Oh, I never thought you were too old for me. Young studs never did anything for me. Who needs it? I've always been partial to more mature men.

TERENCE: Is that right? That's interesting.

ANGIE: Probably because I matured somewhat prematurely myself.

TERENCE: Yes. Probably. No doubt—that explains it.

ANGIE: Matter of fact, I almost asked you out.

TERENCE: You're kidding.

ANGIE: More than once. There was this one time we were in your office talking about my term paper about Grendel in "Beowulf"? And I was wearing this blouse and it was unbuttoned about down to here? Remember that afternoon?

TERENCE: Ahh . . . vaguely.

ANGIE: I came close that afternoon.

TERENCE: Interesting. Isn't it interesting to compare notes like this, long after the fact? Proust has an episode in *Sodom and Gomorrah* where he talks about . . .

ANGIE: What would you have done if I'd asked you out that day?

TERENCE: I probably would have said, "Thank you very much, Miss Graziano, but I'm married." And you would have said, "Oh, I'm sorry, I had no *idea* you were married." And then—

ANGIE: Oh, I knew you were married. It was just obvious that you weren't happily married.

TERENCE: Why was that so obvious?

ANGIE: Because you don't spend an hour and a half locked in your office late on a Friday afternoon looking down a girl's blouse if you're happily married to your wife. Seems elementary to me. You still married, by the way?

TERENCE: Yes, still married.

ANGIE: To the same woman?

TERENCE: The same woman.

ANGIE: Then obviously I was wrong. Obviously you were happy, or why would you still be married, right?

TERENCE: People stay married for lots of different reasons.

ANGIE: Oh sure, but the bottom line is being happy.

TERENCE: Not necessarily.

ANGIE: No? Then what?

TERENCE: Well, sometimes people simply give up. And passively accept their fate.

ANGIE: To me that would be worse than death.

TERENCE: But then you're a lot younger than I am, aren't you?

ANGIE: Age has nothing to do with it. "Never say never," that's my philosophy. (*Enter* LOU, TINO *and* MIKE. TINO, *in his 50s, is a real estate developer, soberly dressed; he is a man of few words and fewer social graces.* MIKE, *a little older, is a more exotic Sicilian wearing dark glasses and an abundance of flashy gold chains; he is suspicious and irritable and he suffers from chronic indigestion. We overhear the tail end of a conversation as they enter*)

MIKE: And the son of a bitch paid 14.40. I could of cut my throat! Hello, Angie . . .

ANGIE: Hi, Uncle Mike.

LOU: Professor, meet my associate, Mike Francisco. Mike, this is Terence O'Keefe. (*They shake hands*)

TERENCE: Mr. Francisco.

MIKE (*offering two fingers*): Nice to meet you.

TINO: Angie—

ANGIE: Uncle Tino.

LOU: And this is Tino, another one of my business associates who's very interested in your proposal. Tino De Felice, Professor O'Keefe.

TERENCE (*shaking hands*): Pleased to meet you.

TINO: How are you?

LOU: So let's all sit down and have a cocktail, something to eat. Mike, try the antipasto. Angel, bring another plate for Mike. Whataya gonna have to drink? You want some wine? Shall we have some red?

MIKE: Nah, I don't want nutting, Louie.

TINO: He don't feel good. He got problems with his stomach.

LOU: A glass of the red'll fix you right up, Mike.

MIKE: Nah, I don't want nutting.

LOU: Bring two plates anyway and a bottle of red and some glasses.

ANGIE: You want to order now, or you wanna wait?

LOU: First bring the red. And another side of fish and rice. You try the fish and rice yet, Professor?

TERENCE: It's very good.

LOU: Try some of the fish anyway, Mike. It's nice, nice little sauce, easy on the stomach.

MIKE: Nah, I don't think so. I don't want nutting. Maybe some soup. What's the soup today?

LOU: What's the soup today, Angel?

ANGIE: I don't know, I have to see.

LOU: But bring the wine first. Is Joey coming?

TINO: I dunno, I couldn't get hold of him.

LOU: Maybe we'll wait to see for Joey to eat, Angel.

ANGIE: Fine, okay. Here's the wine and I'll check on the soup. *(She goes out)*

LOU *(to MIKE)*: You should try the fish, it's good for you.

MIKE: Nah, I don't think so.

LOU: It's probably just gas.

MIKE: I'll have some soup, that's all, and a glass of red. *(To TERENCE)* Lou, he eats and drinks anything he wants. Me? I gotta be careful.

TERENCE: Right. Right. I know what you mean.

MIKE: Lou, he don't worry about nutting. *(He is very suspicious of* TERENCE *and* TERENCE *is nervous; he tries too hard to ingratiate himself)*

LOU: Why should I worry? Life's too short to worry. Let other people worry. Whaddaya get for worrying? Gas on your stomach, right, Professor?

TERENCE: Right. Right! Absolutely!

MIKE *(lifting his glass in a toast):* So, Professor, break your legs!

TERENCE: Huh?

MIKE *(explaining smugly to the others):* That's the way they talk in show business. It's bad luck to say good luck, so instead they say break your legs. It's got a nice ring to it, huh?

TERENCE: Actually, they say, "Break *a* leg."

MIKE: If breaking one leg is good, breaking two is better.

TERENCE: In Europe they say "shit."

MIKE: Where in Europe do they say this, Professor? And why?

TERENCE: In European theatre, in Belgium, for example. "Good shit," actually. Or they hold up their fingers like this—*(He gestures with his hand, five fingers extended, palm upraised)* It means good luck. Only like Mike says, you can't say good luck because that's bad luck, so you say shit, or do like this with your fingers, one finger for each letter.

MIKE: "Shit" has only *four* letters where I come from.

TERENCE: Yeah, but in French it's five.

MIKE *(distrustfully):* Shit has five letters in French? This is news to me.

TINO: The French always have to do things different. Remember Frenchie Carbone?

LOU: God, who could ever forget Frenchie Carbone?

MIKE: Frenchie Carbone! May he rest in peace. *(The three friends make the sign of the cross)* I didn't know he was French.

LOU: Why do you think they called him Frenchie? 'Cause he was Greek?

MIKE: Yeah, but Carbone ain't French.

LOU: He was French on his mother's side.

MIKE: Ah, this explains it. What was his mother's name?

LOU: Mary. His father's name was Joseph.

MIKE: Mary and Joseph don't sound all that French to me.

TINO: Me neither.

LOU: He's French. He's Greek. What do I give a shit?

MIKE: The whole thing seems questionable. Anyway, I prefer "Break your legs," Professor.

TERENCE: Anything you want, Mike.

MIKE: Good. So let's get down to business. This is all very pleasant, but we didn't come here for pleasure.

TERENCE: Right, okay. Well. I don't know how much Lou has told you about my play. But . . .

MIKE *(interrupting)*: Obviously, we don't know nutting about plays, Professor. You're a professor, is that correct? This is why everyone calls you that?

TERENCE: I teach at the State University. This semester I'm on leave.

MIKE: I never graduated grade school myself.

TERENCE: No kidding!

MIKE: Never think it to look at me, huh?

TERENCE: No, God, no!

MIKE: Seventh grade was as far as I made it. And look at me today—worth twenty million, give or take five or ten, right, Tino? *(He gives a laugh that sounds as though he's being strangled. There's a silence)* You probably notice that when I laugh I don't move my lips.

TERENCE: You don't?

MIKE: You didn't notice?

TERENCE: No, I didn't notice anything.

MIKE: You're not very observant. Problem of these muscles, you look close you can see the scars. Go ahead, take a look.

TERENCE *(peering uncomfortably):* Ah, yes. But I wouldn't have noticed if you hadn't—

MIKE: Got slashed. Carved up. Years ago. They did a job on me, right, Louie? Blood all over, you couldn't believe.

LOU: But you shoulda seen the other guy, right, Tino?

MIKE: Ah, well, boys will be boys, right, Professor? *(And he makes the same appalling sound)* Anyway, that's why my lips don't move when I laugh.

TERENCE: That's . . . amazing.

MIKE: But that's the great thing about America, ask Domenic, remember Domenic? Old Domenic, he'd tell you how poor we were, right, Louie? We came here we had nutting, we had shit. But this is the land of opportunity. You start out shit, you end up being President. Look at Reagan. Frank Sinatra. Mario Andretti. Take your pick. You ask me, the next President will be Mario Cuomo. And why not? What's wrong with that? You don't like this idea, Professor?

TERENCE: No, no, no! I love the idea! I'm a big fan of Mario Cuomo, I'd vote for Mario Cuomo in a minute.

MIKE: If not Mario Cuomo, maybe Tommy Lasorda.

TERENCE: I think Tommy Lasorda would make a wonderful President.

MIKE: Who knows? In life you never can know, right, Tino?

TINO: In death neither, Mike.

MIKE: That's true, that's very true. In death neither. *Salud! (Enter* ANGIE *with antipasto, bread and risotto)*

ANGIE: The soup's escarole, Uncle Mike.

MIKE: Okay, bring me a bowl the escarol', Angie.

ANGIE: Uncle Tino?

TINO: I don't know—*(They cross to the table and sit down)*

ANGIE: How about the primavera? That's good.

TINO: I had primavera yesterday. How's the calamar'? Nice and fresh?

LOU *(indignant):* Naturally they're nice and fresh! Whatsa matter with you? The calamar' are always fresh!

TINO: Not always.

LOU: They come in this morning.

TINO: Okay. Then bring me some calamar'. Pasta on the side.

LOU: What about you, Professor? Why don't you try the scallopini? Believe me when I tell you, it's a specialty of the house. Veal so tender you can cut it with your fork. Some spinach on the side? Whataya say?

ANGIE: It's nice, Terence, you'll love it.

TERENCE: Great, I love veal.

LOU: You never had veal.

TERENCE: Probably not. But what I had that was called veal was very good.

LOU: *This* is veal, never mind what you had they called veal! Bring him the veal, Angel.

MIKE: Maybe after all I'll take some calamar' too, Angel. Just a small portion. They ain't too oily, huh? Nice and light?

LOU *(indignant):* Whataya mean oily? The calamar' are always nice and light, whatsa matter with you?

MIKE: Tell the cook, Angie, okay? My stomach's killing me. Tell 'em to go easy with the grease.

LOU: Whataya talking about *grease?* Since when we serve you a greasy meal around here?

MIKE: Tell the cook, okay, honey? And put some hot pepper in the escarole—not too much, just a touch.

ANGIE: You want something, Dad?

LOU: I think I'll have a bowl of pasta fazzul.

MIKE: That sounds good, Angie. I'll have some fazzul too.

ANGIE: Okay.

MIKE: Nutting like a good plate of fazzul to absorb the acid, Professor. (ANGIE *goes out)*

LOU: How's your drink, Professor?

TERENCE: Fine, it's fine, Lou! Strong!

LOU: Tino, try the fish.

TINO: I had fish for lunch.

MIKE: So then, what's the deal, Professor? Why don't you show us what you got, using language we can all understand, in not so many words.

TERENCE: Right, okay. *(He delves into his briefcase)* Here, I brought some copies of the script for everybody. And these are the reviews from the Buffalo production and the limited partnership agreements.

MIKE: Wasn't Buffalo Primo's territory? Primo and Domenic?

TINO: Yeah, in the 60s.

MIKE: That's what I thought, they had Buffalo all buttoned up between them for a while. Then they got greedy. Greed's a terrible thing, Professor.

TERENCE: Terrible!

MIKE: Poor old Domenic, he got too big for his britches, may he rest in peace. *(They all cross themselves)* Go ahead, Professor, don't let me interrupt you. You say these are the limited partnership papers. Fine. Our legal staff will look into these.

LOU: Why don't you tell us about your play, Terence?

MIKE: Terence? Your name is Terence?

TERENCE: Yes, Terence. Terence O'Keefe.

MIKE: Call you Terence?

TERENCE: Fine, great! Why not? That is my name, after all.

MIKE: Dispense with the formalities, it's better that way.

TERENCE *(continuing throughout in ecstasies of servility):* I couldn't agree more, Mike. Call you Mike? Lots better that way.

MIKE *(chillingly):* Only my intimates call me Mike.

TERENCE: Oh, sorry, of course, sure, presumptuous of me, wasn't it, sir? Mister. Mister . . . uh . . .

MIKE: But lucky for you I view you as an intimate. *(And he gives his ghastly laugh)* Incidentally, I got nutting whatsoever against the Irish, in case you're wondering.

TERENCE: It truly never crossed my mind.

MIKE: It *should* have crossed your mind, you shouldn't ever take nutting for granted, Terence.

TINO: So let Terence tell us about his play.

MIKE: Right, shoot, Terence. What's the subject of this play of yours?

TERENCE: The subject is crime, actually.

MIKE: Crime?

TERENCE: Yes, crime. It's about *a* crime, you see—you'll see it when you read the script or even these reviews if you don't feel like reading the script. The reviews give you a pretty good idea of the story line.

MIKE: Let's hear it in your own words, Terence. Make me want to invest in your play.

TERENCE: Well, it's about a murder. See, it's kind of a cross between *Sleuth* and *Deathtrap.* Sort of an intellectual cross between Peter Shaffer and Anthony Shaffer.

MIKE: Are we familiar with these gentlemen?

TINO: They're top of the line, Mike. Very successful.

MIKE: At what?

TERENCE: They're playwrights, actually.

MIKE: And what you're saying, Terence, you are ripping off these gavones?

TERENCE: I confess to an influence there, yes, certainly.

LOU: Mike, what he means is that he's operating in the same territory.

MIKE: And in your business they permit this, to encroach on the territory of the competition?

TERENCE: It's not only permitted, it's encouraged.

MIKE: I find this very interesting.

TERENCE: But of course at the same time my play is completely original. I mean, in another sense I don't owe anything to anybody. Because it's a play where you get into the psychology of the killer. I mean, the audience actually participates in the crime. In a way, in fact, it's the audience that's guilty in the last analysis. You see, the play deals with universal guilt and the theme of man's responsibility for his fellow man. Which may sound a little too intellectual, perhaps, but really, up in Buffalo, it was . . .

MIKE *(interrupting):* I saw Ethel Merman once. Live.

TERENCE *(brought up short):* What? You saw who?

MIKE: Ethel Merman. A very great actress.

TERENCE *(after a pause):* Oh God, yes, she certainly was. One of the greatest.

MIKE: In *Desert Song.*

TERENCE: *Desert Song?* I don't think Ethel Merman was ever *in*—(MIKE *stops him with a bleak glance. Hastily shifting gears)* Though it's possible, naturally. It's just that I wasn't *aware* she'd ever. . . . But, I mean, she certainly *could* have played in *The Desert Song.* Why not? I bet she was terrific.

MIKE: Saw her in the Candlelight, down on the shore. Old summer theatre. Remember that tent they used to have, Louie?

LOU: What tent? I don't remember no tent.

MIKE: The tent where I saw Ethel Merman, summer of '52. In *The Desert Song*. With Ezio Pinza. Had the time of my life.

TERENCE: No, now wait a minute! Wait a minute! Ethel Merman, maybe. But Ezio Pinza? Come on, get out of here, Mike. Not Ezio Pinza, not in a million years!

MIKE: Ezio Pinza was a cousin of mine.

TERENCE: On the other hand, what do I know? It was before my time. Why not Ezio Pinza? Why not Callas? Why not Caruso?

MIKE: A *distant* cousin. Three or four times removed. On my mother's side, God bless her. A great gift, Ezio Pinza, a very great talent.

TERENCE: Oh, absolutely, no question about it. One of the best!

MIKE: And very religious, did you know that?

TERENCE: No, actually, I didn't know that.

MIKE: Very religious. Used to go to mass every day.

TERENCE: Really? No kidding. Imagine that.

MIKE: I never go to church myself. Except for funerals and baptisms. But I don't like people making fun of religion.

TERENCE: I don't blame you. Some things ought to be sacred. Religion is certainly one of them.

MIKE: What about Don Ameche?

TERENCE *(thrown for a moment by the non sequitur):* Don Ameche?

MIKE: There's a great talent for you too. A man years before his time.

TERENCE: Actually he was before mine too. Though I've only ever heard the very finest things about him.

MIKE: I saw Don Ameche on "The Johnny Carson Show" last winter. Looked great, in great shape for a guy 83, or 84, whatever he was.

LOU: I thought he was dead.

MIKE: Then he was in *really* great shape on "The Johnny Carson Show"! *(And he gives his ghastly laugh)* So. Terence. If this play of yours is such a hot item, how come you gotta raise the money from amateurs like us?

TERENCE: I anticipated that question.

MIKE: Then you probably got a good answer.

TERENCE: You use the word "amateur." Which is just the right word. It means "lover." From the Latin: "Amo, amas, amat." One who loves something. And I think it's time we took commercial theatre out of the hands of the professionals and put it into the hands of the amateurs, the true lovers of art. As in the Renaissance, for example, when your great princely families were in the strictest and best sense of the word "amateurs." If theatre is to survive we have to return to the traditions of the Medici family, for example, who . . .

MIKE: You know the Medicis?

TERENCE: Yes, of course, I mean, who doesn't?

MIKE: They were into show business too?

TERENCE: They were into everything even remotely related to the arts.

MIKE: This is news to me. I thought they were into booze and prostitution.

TINO: And horses too, they used to run horses down at Gulfstream in the winter.

TERENCE: I'm sorry . . . we seem not to be talking about the same Medicis.

MIKE: We're talking about Carlo and Jimmie Medici outa Worcester, Mass. Who you talking about?

TERENCE: Another branch of the family.

MIKE: Well, it was a big family. Very big family.

TERENCE: Yes, prolific.

MIKE: Whatever. Like I said before, we don't know nutting about plays. So the way I see it, what you're asking us to do is invest in you personally, that's what it comes down to, am I right or wrong?

TERENCE: In a sense, yes, I guess that's so.

MIKE: But naturally we don't know nutting about you either. So it's a crap shoot.

LOU: Hey, Mike, it ain't exactly a crap shoot.

MIKE: A crap shoot I don't mind. I shoot craps. I love to shoot craps. I'm only trying to characterize the enterprise for what it is in so many words stripped of all illusions, Louie, that's all I'm trying to do.

LOU: Right. I understand. But it ain't a crap shoot. They did Terry's play already and it was a big hit in Buffalo. You got the play, you got the reviews, you got a star who agrees to play the part.

MIKE: Who is this star? Why have I never heard of this star?

LOU: Who the hell knows why you never heard of this star? The whole world knows him. You don't! All you know is Ezio Pinza. What am I supposed to do, drop dead because you never heard of this star?

MIKE: What's his name?

LOU: How the hell do I know what his name is? He's a star.

MIKE: Okay, I'm ready to take your word on it. You say he's a star, he's a star. Fine, okay, but let's understand one thing right off the bat, Professor. We ain't interested in making six percent off our investment. We lose a hundred grand, two hundred grand, okay, so what? It ain't the first time, it won't be the last time. But if we win, I want to win big. I want to make six percent on my money, I'll put it into stocks and bonds, I'll buy C's and D's, you follow me, Professor?

LOU: We're interested in the action, Terry, you see what I'm saying? We're not afraid to take a plunge as long as we realize there's the possibility of a score.

TINO: Then, why are we talking *Off*-Broadway? If this property is such a gold mine, why ain't we talking Broadway?

MIKE: Why ain't we talking Don Ameche and Ida Lupino? Lemme ask you this. How much does it cost to do this play right? Everything top shelf. One million? Two million?

TERENCE: Around $800,000. Maybe nine.

MIKE: So why are we fooling around with nickels and dimes? You have confidence in Terry, Lou, you're familiar with his career over the years?

LOU: I've know him since Angie was in college with him taking his class. He's been close before. One of his plays was a big hit in Belgium. I think he's ripe.

MIKE: That's good enough for me. So then why don't we take the whole thing? Never mind limited partnerships and all the rest of them technicalities. We're gonna plunge, Louie, why don't we *plunge?*

LOU: Hey, I give a shit, it's up to you. Whatever you want's okay with me.

TERENCE: You mean you guys are going to invest nine hundred thousand dollars in my play? My play? Are you crazy?

MIKE: Well, naturally we have to read your play first, Terence.

LOU: Or we'll have Angie read it.

TINO: Or whoever.

MIKE: And then we'll talk things over among ourselves and our partners and make our decision accordingly.

TERENCE: You'll probably hate it. You'll probably think it's just a silly academic exercise by an ivory tower intellectual.

LOU: Nobody came here to hate your play, Terry. (ANGIE *enters with their food on a large tray*)

ANGIE: Here you are, Uncle Mike. This'll fix you up in no time.

MIKE: You got an agent or whatever, Terence? I suppose you're gonna want something in writing.

TERENCE: Well, yes, eventually, that would be nice.

MIKE: Normally, with us our word is our bond. We shake hands, the deal is done. But I can see maybe you wouldn't be comfortable working on that basis.

TERENCE: Oh, I don't care. A handshake would be fine with me. But my agent gets nervous about these things.

ANGIE: Frankie Salvucci's here.

MIKE: Oh yeah? Good. Happy to see him.

LOU: You know, Mike, this Frankie. Somebody gotta do something. Bruno saw him over at OTB yesterday. Says he dropped two, three grand.

TINO: Two, three grand!

LOU: He owes this guy, he owes that guy. Ten grand here, ten grand there. First he was gonna pay us in two weeks—then it was three months. Now we're on seven months. Come on, Mike, we gotta do something about this guy.

MIKE: Hey, he ain't got the money we tell him, hey, Frankie, HEY! You know what I mean? Kidding is kidding, but this ain't kidding! (FRANKIE SALVUCCI *enters, a pale, nervous, beaten little man trying to maintain a front of false heartiness and joviality*)

FRANKIE: Hey, Angie!

ANGIE: Hi, Uncle Frankie.

FRANKIE: Louie!

LOU: Hello, Frankie.

FRANKIE: Tino, Mike.

MIKE: Hullo, Frankie.

LOU: Frankie, meet Terence O'Keefe. Frankie Salvucci. Terence used to be Angie's teacher at the university.

FRANKIE: Hello, Terence.

TERENCE: Pleasure.

LOU: Angel, bring Frankie a chair, sit down, Frankie. Whataya gonna have to drink?

FRANKIE: No, no, no, it's okay, nothing, really, I can't stay. (ANGIE *brings a chair*) Well, okay. Thanks, Angie. Okay, bring me a . . . a scotch, double scotch, Angie. (ANGIE *exits*)

LOU: Terence here has written a play we're thinking of investing in.

FRANKIE: Well, I can come back, I don't want to interrupt anything . . .

LOU: We're all friends, Frankie, you ain't interrupting nothing.

MIKE: You're looking good, Frankie. You're looking very good. The wife's taking care of you, and how is the little woman anyway?

FRANKIE: Fine, fine, she's just fine, Mike. Sends you and Rose her regards.

MIKE: I'll convey them to Rose, she'll be very pleased. She was just saying the other day, "Why don't we ever see Lena and Frankie anymore, I miss them."

FRANKIE: That was nice. Lena misses her too. *(He lights a cigarette)*

MIKE: Don't he look good, Louie? Nice color to his face.

LOU: Very nice color, you working out, Frankie?

FRANKIE: Oh, you know, a little squash time to time, little handball.

TINO: Cigarettes'll be the death of you yet, Frankie boy!

FRANKIE: Ah, what the hell, Tino! Gotta have some vices, huh? (ANGIE *returns with the drink)*

ANGIE: Here you are, Uncle Frankie.

FRANKIE: Thanks, Angie. . . . *(He drains the glass nervously)* Hey, what's this I hear about you getting married?

ANGIE: Married! Where you buying your information? You should get your money back, Uncle Frankie.

FRANKIE: No, but I heard that, seriously, I don't remember who told me, Nickie or somebody, I can't remember who, but somebody definitely told me you were getting married.

LOU: She's my baby—she's got plenty of time to get married.

FRANKIE: Joanna's getting married, you know.

ANGIE: Joanna!? Really? No kidding. Joanna who?

FRANKIE: Bennie's kid Joanna.

ANGIE: Oh yeah!

FRANKIE: Yeah, you believe it? Little Joanna. To a kid she met in college.

LOU: Is he Italian?

FRANKIE: I don't know. Funny you should ask, but I just don't know. I would imagine. Wouldn't you think so, Mike? I would certainly imagine she'd marry an Italian. You know Bennie, he'd go through the roof. Still, the world's changing. Whataya gonna do? Things have to change. All these Orientals come over since Vietnam, take my Christina, she brings these little Koreans over the house to play. Who's to say she grows up she ain't gonna marry some Chink? And what am I supposed to do, *disown* her? My own flesh and blood? It's the times, you gotta be flexible. Anyway, God bless you, honey, and best of luck, you just listen to your own heart and let your conscience be your guide.

ANGIE: Nice to see you again, Uncle Frankie. Tell Aunt Lena and Christina hello from me. (ANGIE *leaves. There's a silence*)

LOU: Try some of the fish and rice, Frankie.

FRANKIE: No, I already ate, thanks, Lou.

MIKE: Nice to see you again, looking so good and full of healthy color, Frankie. You say you're playing squash and handball?

FRANKIE: Yeah, you know, Mike, I'm not a fanatic or nothing, but time to time . . .

MIKE: You get to be our age, nutting more important than to stay in shape.

TINO: We were getting worried about you, Frankie. Thought maybe you'd left town.

LOU: Without saying goodbye. This made us sad, Frankie.

FRANKIE (*with a weak laugh*): Why would I leave town? I got no reason to leave town.

MIKE: Glad to hear it. We're all glad to hear it. Because to tell you the truth, we were beginning to feel a little. . . . What's the word I'm looking for, Tino?

TINO: Apprehensive.

MIKE: Exactly the word I was looking for.

LOU: What Mike's driving at, Frankie, is we were under the impression that we were supposed to conclude our business with you two weeks ago. Maybe I was mistaken about the date, but that was my impression.

MIKE: Anyway, what's the difference, one week, two weeks? We're all friends. We're not talking strangers who don't trust each other, we're talking friends, almost family, after all. The important thing is Frankie's here.

TERENCE *(who has been feeling more and more uncomfortable):* Uh, maybe . . . if you have business to discuss, I can, I have some phone calls I can make, and uh—

LOU *(reasonably):* Relax, Terence, it's no big deal.

FRANKIE: No, but maybe, if we *could* talk in private a few minutes, fellows.

MIKE: Nutting you can't say openly in front of the Professor, Frankie. All friends, all in the family, we got nutting to hide, right, Professor? *(And he gives his ghastly, chilling laugh again. There's a silence)*

TINO: So then, why don't we just wrap this up then, Frankie?

MIKE: You bring Frankie's note?

TINO: Right here.

MIKE: Never mind the interest on the late charges, what is it, maybe we were wrong anyway about the date, Louie says maybe we got it wrong, Frankie, anyway we're all friends, right?

LOU: So here's your note, you give us the money and we'll have a drink.

FRANKIE: Yeah, well, unfortunately, see . . .

TINO: What is it, Frankie?

MIKE: Frankie's obviously got something on his mind. What is it, Frankie?

FRANKIE (*feebly, pleading hopelessly*): I need more time.

LOU: More time . . .

FRANKIE: Another week, just another week, one more week . . .

TINO (*shaking his head*): Frankie, Frankie, Frankie . . .

MIKE: Do I understand correctly you're all jammed up?

FRANKIE: Just another week, I swear, I'll have it in one more week, so help me God.

MIKE: Frankie, relax! Hey, who doesn't get jammed up time to time? Everybody gets jammed up, I get jammed up, the professor, Lou, we all get jammed up.

We're all friends here, a circle of friends, Tino, Mike, Frankie, Lou, Terence.

FRANKIE: It's like you say, Mike. I . . . uh . . . I'm jammed up. I just need a little more time. Another week or two.

LOU: A week or *two* now, Frankie?

FRANKIE: Hey, you know I'm good for it! What am I gonna do, leave town? You guys always know where to find me.

TERENCE *(alarmed and embarrassed):* Really, I have some errands I can run, no problem. I'll be back in an hour, hour and a half.

MIKE: Wait a minute, Terence, it's all right, it's okay.

TERENCE: No, Mike, I'd feel a lot better if . . .

MIKE: But we're all through here, our business with Frankie's concluded.

FRANKIE: It is?

MIKE: Naturally, whataya think we are? A friend's jammed up, needs more time to get his affairs in order, what am I supposed to do? I'm a reasonable man, Frankie, you know that. Lou is reasonable. Tino is— well, Tino is maybe less reasonable than me and Louie, but he's not unreasonable, right, Tino? Hey, Frankie!—*(He puts one arm around* FRANKIE's *neck, draws him into an embrace, slaps his face lightly)* You know what you are, Frankie? You're a goofball. Ain't he a goofball, Lou? *(He laughs)*

LOU: He certainly ain't no rocket scientist.

MIKE: You object to being called a goofball?

FRANKIE *(with a false laugh):* I been called worse than that, Mike, in my time, as well you know. Been called worse by *him.* *(This last sheepishly to* TERENCE*)*

MIKE: Okay, okay, go on home, goofball. And don't worry about this note. You see how worried I am, Frankie? This is how worried I am about this note? *(And he takes the note and lights a match and burns it. They all watch it go up in flames in silence)*

FRANKIE: I really appreciate this, Mike.

MIKE: Nutting.

FRANKIE: I'll never forget this, never. I'll pay you guys back every penny, every penny! With interest!

MIKE: Nutting, nutting, nutting!

FRANKIE: Two weeks. Three weeks. Maximum three weeks.

TINO: Okay, that's enough; beat it, Frankie.

MIKE: God love you, goofball.

FRANKIE: Goodnight, Professor, Tino . . . Lou.

LOU *(seated):* Yeah, get the hell outta here.

FRANKIE: Okay, so long then. *(He leaves uncertainly. The others watch him go, then without a word,* TINO *and* MIKE *follow.* TERENCE *is startled)*

TERENCE: Is . . . is something wrong, Lou?

LOU *(innocently, lighting a cigar):* What makes you ask, Terence?

TERENCE: I don't know. Did they leave?

LOU: Probably just went to the john. Mike's got a prostrate problem, he pees a lot. I'll go check 'em out. Won't be a minute, Terry. Enjoy! *(And he leaves. Terence is very uneasy. He drinks his drink, picks at some of the food. A great sense of isolation. Then* ANGIE *enters with more bread)*

ANGIE: Hey, all alone? Where is everybody?

TERENCE: They went to the toilet.

ANGIE: All of them? Simultaneously.

TERENCE: So I was told.

ANGIE: What's the matter?

TERENCE: Nothing. Why?

ANGIE: You look like . . . something's the matter.

TERENCE: No, it's just, just a little strange. This Frankie, this Uncle Frankie. . . . Are they *all* your uncles?

ANGIE: No, I just call them that, I call everybody Uncle Vito, Aunt Clara. I guess some of them are related to me in actuality and some of them aren't.

TERENCE: He seemed to be in some kind of trouble.

ANGIE: Frankie? Ah, he's always in some kind of trouble. He was born in some kind of trouble. Never mind Frankie. What do they say? He's the sort who always lands on his feet.

TERENCE: But he seemed to be frightened, really frightened.

ANGIE: The thing about these guys you have to understand, Terence, you gotta take everything they say with a grain of salt. They're overgrown kids, that's all. Retarded adolescents. How's your drink? Can I freshen your drink?

TERENCE: Yes, please.

ANGIE: We're all out of tonic. Be right back. *(She leaves. He takes his scripts and starts to leave. She returns with a drink)* There you are. See, the thing about Frankie, you don't understand Italians. They always have to force things. That's how we are. It's all very dramatic. They think if they behave like something they want has already happened, then it *will* happen. Like about me getting married. Nobody told Frankie I was getting married. He just made that up because he *wants* me to get married. *(She delivers drink to* TER-ENCE*)*

TERENCE: Thanks. But what's it to him if you get married?

ANGIE: What's it to anybody? That's what I'm telling you! You gotta take these things with a grain of salt. *(She sits down and kicks off her shoes)* Oh, God, my feet are killing me. I may be rich before I'm forty, but I'm gonna have fallen arches, too. You mind if I just elevate 'em like that for a few minutes? *(And she puts her feet in his lap)*

TERENCE: No, not at all.

ANGIE *(wiggling):* Ah, God, that feels good. *(He lets out a whinnying cry of laughter)*

TERENCE: That tickles!

ANGIE: You don't mind massaging them just a little?

TERENCE: No, I don't mind. *(He begins to massage her left foot)*

ANGIE: Oh, Jesus! Mmmmmmm! *(She wiggles in her chair voluptuously; since her foot is in his lap, he wiggles in response and begins massaging more vigorously)* You've really got quite a touch—for an intellectual.

TERENCE *(self-consciously releasing her):* Is that enough?

ANGIE *(giving him an excited kick in the stomach):* Don't stop! *(He resumes)*

TERENCE: I guess they really hurt, huh? *(Her eyes are closed. She only emits small groans and sighs of contentment)* People never stop to think about how in a job like this, how difficult it is, the effect it has just on your posture, standing on your feet, erect all day.

ANGIE: That's really good, Terence! Mmm, God, that's wonderful!

TERENCE *(babbling):* And I suppose working for yourself, being self-employed and everything, you probably don't even have Blue Cross and Blue Shield, let alone major medical . . .

ANGIE: Faster, Terence, harder, don't stop! *(He is now evidently quite aroused himself; he has no idea of what he's saying)*

TERENCE: I'm always getting into trouble myself with the IRS because of the Self-employment Tax, they're always arguing that my business is really just a hobby— so I'm not entitled to deduct my—*(He suddenly stops, arrested by something he sees out the window)* But, there's your dad in the alley with Frankie and Tino and Mike.

ANGIE: Don't stop! *(He resumes automatically, but stares with developing horror at what's transpiring outside the window)* Ohhhhhh!

TERENCE: But what are they *doing* to Frankie?

ANGIE: Who *cares* what they're doing? Fixing Frankie's car.

TERENCE: Frankie's car!

ANGIE: Oh God! (*Her back stiffens, her head falls back as though she's in a faint, her skirt rides up on her thighs as her legs fall open. Terence doesn't know what to do; simultaneously, she seems to be having either an orgasm or an epileptic fit; he is very aroused himself and is terrified someone may enter the room at any moment and discover them; and outside in the alley, he is seeing something unbelievably terrible and outrageous going on. Angie writhes and thrashes. Terence continues massaging her foot as though he were masturbating. She is groaning and gasping. He keeps trying to pull her skirt down over her knees, without success. And all the time he keeps shifting his attention back and forth between her and what's happening in the alley*)

TERENCE: Oh, my God!

ANGIE: Oh, God, Terence! Don't stop!

TERENCE: But what are they doing to Frankie?

ANGIE: Never mind Frankie. (*He starts to rise, but she kicks him in the stomach and he sits down abruptly again*) Don't stop, don't stop.

TERENCE: But God Almighty, oh no! Oh Jesus! Oh fuck!

ANGIE: Ohh, Mmmm! Ohhhhh! Aahhhh! *(And* ANGIE *gives a prolonged ecstatic shriek and topples from her chair. Without releasing her foot, Terence jumps up and stands like that, gaping out of the window, clutching* ANGIE'*s foot to his breast as, on her back, legs straight up in the air,* ANGIE *grinds, pumps and shudders.* TERENCE *gives a climactic cry of nausea and horror at what he sees in the alley and the lights go to black. End of Act One)*

Act II

ACT II

Scene One

The same, the next day. LOU *is reading the newspaper,* MIKE *is pacing irritably up and down.*

LOU: Where did they dig up this picture of Frankie? Looks like his high school graduation.

MIKE: Frankie never graduated high school, may he rest in peace.

LOU: They did a very nice job with the obituary. I didn't know his mother was still alive.

MIKE: How old is she?

LOU: It don't say. She must be a hundred and five. What about your old lady? She must be near a hundred by now.

MIKE: Ninety-seven. How old is yours?

LOU: Ninety-four, ninety-five, I dunno. Who counts. Ninety-six, ninety-seven . . .

MIKE: Anyway, God bless her.

LOU: God bless all of 'em, I just wish they wouldn't talk so much. Here's a horse in the seventh at Hialeah named Frankie Boy!

MIKE: Don't even think about it.

LOU: He's a long shot, forty to one, Mike!

MIKE: Forget it, whatasa matter with you?

LOU: How can I not bet a horse named Frankie Boy that's forty-to-one on a day like this?

MIKE *(sternly):* Show some respect! There are some things you just don't do for money.

LOU *(reluctantly):* Yeah, you're right, you're right.

MIKE: Be serious, Louie.

LOU: Okay, okay. But if that horse comes in . . . ! Fangul!

MIKE: Where the hell's Tino? We can't do nutting without Tino.

LOU: He's over talking to Frankie's wife.

MIKE: It's a tragedy, a terrible tragedy. You ever stop and think, Louie, what's it all mean? There's Frankie Salvucci, snuffed out before his time, hit by a train, the 9:02 from Boston. You get what I'm getting at?

Finer human being than Frankie Salvucci . . . you follow me, Lou?

LOU: It's a tragedy, like you say. Mike, the horse is forty-to-one!

MIKE: Will you *stop* about that horse? What about this bird, Terence?

LOU: What about him?

MIKE: Well, he's a college professor, right? Who can predict how a character like that is going to react to a tragedy like this?

LOU: What the hell you saying, Mike? How's he supposed to react? A tragedy's a tragedy.

MIKE: I don't like it, that's all I'm saying.

LOU: You don't like it! What's there to like? He didn't even know Frankie Salvucci.

MIKE: That's what I mean. Maybe he don't share our feelings about this tragic accident that happened to a man we all knew and loved like my own brother.

LOU: Naturally he shares our feelings. What? He's not human?

MIKE: He's a college professor!

LOU: College professors have feelings too.

MIKE: You read his play yet?

LOU: When am I supposed to read his play?

MIKE: I think we better read it.

LOU: You read it.

MIKE: Might give us a better idea who we're dealing with, Louie, that's all I'm saying.

LOU: I know who we're dealing with.

MIKE: You know, I don't.

LOU: So read his play. What do I give a shit?

MIKE: Somebody's got to read it, anyway, sooner or later.

LOU: Why?

MIKE: We're gonna back this show, it might be a good idea to have some idea what the hell we're backing.

LOU: Mike, you're the one with problems. I got no problems. I believe in this show, I believe in Terence. I don't have to read nothing. I think you're barking up the wrong tree. He wants to do business with us!

MIKE: I ain't convinced. How do we know we can trust him? Is he Catholic?

LOU: How the hell do I know if he's Catholic? He's Irish.

MIKE: Being Irish used to mean something when we were kids. It don't mean nutting anymore, Louie, you know that as well as I do.

LOU: Hey, it make you feel any better we'll baptize him. You can be the godfather. *(Enter* ANGIE*)*

ANGIE: Hi, Dad, Uncle Mike. *(They kiss)*

MIKE: Hello, Angel.

ANGIE: Poor Uncle Frankie, huh?

MIKE: May he rest in peace, Angie. *(He and* LOU *make the sign of the cross)*

ANGIE: I been saying for years there was gonna be an accident at that crossing. Who needs trains anyway, this day and age? People want to go to Boston, why can't they fly?

MIKE: Terrible tragedy.

ANGIE: Terrible.

MIKE: Where's the professor?

ANGIE: I was just talking to him. He's gonna come over after a while.

MIKE: He read the thing about Frankie?

ANGIE: Yeah, he's very upset.

MIKE: How upset?

ANGIE: Very upset. He thinks it's . . . it's a terrible, terrible tragedy. He wants to come over and talk about
his play.

LOU (to MIKE *feeling vindicated*): See, what I tell you?

ANGIE: Something to eat, Uncle Mike? Something to
drink?

MIKE: No, my stomach's killing me, Angie, couldn't
touch a thing. You hear about Patsie? They had to
take out his I'm not sure what you call it, his digestive
track, and fix him up with one of them hoses that goes
into a bag and hangs down inside his shorts. Jesus,
gives me the creeps! Maybe a small glass of anisette.
Whataya think, Lou? To soothe the lining? Or some
club soda. Yeah, bring me a big glass of club soda.
And maybe some meatballs. (*Enter* TINO) Tino . . .

TINO: Mike, Lou.

MIKE: Louie says you been condoning with the be-
reaved.

TINO: Yeah, it's rough. You know, I hate this kind of
thing, Mike. I hate it.

MIKE: Naturally, you hate it. What? Are you supposed to
love it? Who doesn't hate such a thing?

TINO: Next time, *you* go.

MIKE: They got enough to eat over there? Let's send some food. They always need food in times like this. People dropping in to make the condolences, they end up eating like animals. Send some sides of beef, cold cuts, cakes, pies, watermelon, whatever they need.

TINO: They got plenty of food; it looks like the A&P in there already.

MIKE: No such thing as too much food. Where's the phone, Lou?

LOU: Over there.

ANGIE: You want something, Dad?

LOU: Naw, nothing, hon. Maybe a steak sandwich. . . . Or maybe some veal and peppers, I don't care.

MIKE: Lou, what's Frankie's number?

LOU: 569-4332.

MIKE *(dialing)*: 569-4332.

LOU: Whataya gonna have, Tino?

TINO: Bring me a beer, Angie.

LOU: Angie, bring Tino a beer. (ANGIE *exits*)

MIKE: Hello, Lena, this is Mike. Love ya, Lena, God bless and may Frankie rest in peace. Just calling to tell you don't worry about a thing, kid, you hear what I'm saying? Nobody in your house is gonna want for nutting. And little Frankie, little Carmen, little— (*Aside to* LOU) What's the girl's name?

LOU: Ave Maria.

MIKE: Little Ave Maria.

TINO: No, it's Gabriella.

MIKE: I mean little Gabriella. (*Aside*) God damn it, make up your mind!

LOU: What do I know? It's one or the other. Try Christina.

MIKE: Your entire little family, Lena, God bless the whole bunch of you, you will want for nutting. Don't worry about the last rites, we're sending over Bennie Bertelli's Funeral Home, free of charge. It's what I'm telling ya, Lena, doll—the funeral's on me! Naturally, whataya think, who you think you're dealing with? Lena, let me tell you, finer human being than your husband . . . I guarantee your kids will go to college, Lena. Take it straight from the mouth of Mike Francisco, so help me God, their future is guaranteed on the grave of my mother, may God strike me dead if it ain't, Lena. Stiff upper lip, Lena, Frankie's with the saints and angels, doll. My pleasure, babe. We'll see you tonight at the wake. Anything you want or need,

don't hesitate, you hear me? Believe me when I tell
you, kid. So long, now. *(He hangs up)*

LOU: How is she?

MIKE: I don't know. Who cares? I want this funeral top
of the line.

LOU: Then why you sending that two-bit crook Bertelli
over there?

MIKE: He owes me a favor.

LOU: He's always cutting corners to save a dime.

MIKE: He's been known to rise to the occasion.

LOU: I'd rather not be buried, than be buried by him.

MIKE: I'll remember that when your time comes. Every-
thing's gotta be top shelf. Get somebody to sing, "I
Did It My Way." It was a sentimental favorite of
Frankie's.

TINO: We can get Giulio, he does a great imitation of
Sinatra.

LOU: Giulio? Giulio's in the can doing three to five.

TINO: I didn't know this.

LOU: Where you been?

MIKE: Anyway, I just remembered, he doesn't do Sinatra. He does Liberace.

TINO: That must go over great in the can.

MIKE: Lou, call Bertelli. Make sure he understands, we want everything top shelf, top drawer, top of the line. Stretch limos for the next of kin. The works. (LOU *dials and keeps dialing, getting busy signals*)

TINO: What about the eulogy?

MIKE: We got our own professor, why can't he write the eulogy?

LOU: Whataya talking about the eulogy? He didn't even know Frankie.

MIKE: Hey, nothing to it. Our dear Brother Frankie. Valley of tears, blessed saints and angels. Occasion not for grief but for rejoicing. A clever guy like him can write a Broadway play, he can do it in his sleep. You can help him. What you don't know, make up.

LOU: No answer. Bertelli's not home.

MIKE (*to* TINO): Why don't you go over there and you tell Bertelli, just impress on Bertelli how it's in his best interests to provide a quality undertaking for the dear departed.

TINO: Right.

MIKE: Remind him of past courtesies extended.

LOU: Right.

MIKE: Take no shit.

TINO: Right. *(He leaves)*

MIKE: Come on, Louie.

LOU: Where we going?

MIKE: To arrange for the catering.

LOU: Why don't I cater?

MIKE: Guy owes me a favor, I can get a better price.

LOU: I'll give you a good price.

MIKE: Can you beat nutting?

(Blackout)

Scene Two

Late at night in the same room of the restaurant. TERENCE *is scribbling furiously, crumpled sheets of paper strewn everywhere. A bottle of whisky and a glass are at his elbow.*

TERENCE: Our dear Brother Frankie . . . not an occasion for grief—but for rejoicing. Rejoicing? *(Tears pa-*

per off and starts again) No. Our dear Brother Frankie
. . . look at it this way . . . even as we speak, is being welcomed into the company of the saints and angels. And isn't this reason for optimism? Because if
Frankie Salvucci is being welcomed by the saints and
the angels, obviously they'll take anybody. *(Trying
again)* He was my friend . . . *(Enter* ANGIE)

ANGIE: Why don't you knock it off? Finish it in the
morning.

TERENCE: The funeral's tomorrow. I have to finish it to
night.

ANGIE: It's only a eulogy. It's not the Gettysburg Ad-
dress. *(She removes her shoe)* God, my feet are killing
me! *(He gives her a horrified look, but she doesn't notice)* Wasn't it a wonderful wake.

TERENCE: Yes. The thing I liked best was the *tableau vi-
vante* of the widow in the arms of Mike's wife. Fabu-
lous comic touch. Could never invent something like
that.

ANGIE: You know, I've been thinking—the way Frankie
smoked cigarettes, he probably didn't have long to
live anyway.

TERENCE: I've never been to a wake before.

ANGIE: You're kidding.

TERENCE: Never been to a wake before.

ANGIE: I thought the Irish were big on wakes.

TERENCE: We weren't ethnic in my family.

ANGIE: We're very ethnic.

TERENCE: I've gleaned that.

ANGIE: You're half sloshed.

TERENCE: I'm trying to get thoroughly sloshed. You know how they embalm a corpse?

ANGIE: You're cute when you're drunk.

TERENCE: No, no, listen. I was talking to the funeral director . . . this Bertelli. Wonderful character. . . . A master of cosmetic art. They insert this kind of suction device into his. . . .

ANGIE *(interrupting):* I really don't think you should dwell on these things.

TERENCE: How can I not dwell on them? I'm writing Frankie's eulogy.

ANGIE: Yeah, but you don't have to be morbid. I think I'll have a nightcap with you.

TERENCE: None of this seems to bother you very much.

ANGIE: I've been going to wakes since I was three years old. I can't believe you've never been before. You looked like part of the family. You looked like you belonged.

TERENCE: Protective coloration. A phenomenon remarkable in certain sub-evolutionary forms of plant and insect life very low on the biological ladder.

ANGIE: I thought we made a very good-looking couple.

TERENCE: You know, when you really stop and think about it, maybe this isn't such a good idea.

ANGIE: What isn't?

TERENCE: My going into business with your dad and his friends. See, they probably have certain expectations that are . . . well, that aren't very realistic. What if they write me a check for a million dollars and . . .

ANGIE: Oh, they never write checks. They'll probably meet you in some alley and hand it over in a paper bag.

TERENCE: But I mean, they don't realize . . . most plays never make a profit. They stand a very good chance of losing all their money!

ANGIE: They lose it, they lose it, no big deal.

TERENCE: Where's all their money come from?

ANGIE *(coldly all of a sudden):* That's none of your business.

TERENCE: No, I only meant that you can't finance a Broadway play with the revenues from this restaurant.

ANGIE: How do you know what this restaurant's worth?

TERENCE: Well, obviously, I don't. But . . .

ANGIE: Or how many restaurants we own? Or what else we're into besides restaurants?

TERENCE: What else are you into?

ANGIE: Maybe we're into laundromats, custodial services, real estate, Tastee Freeze! What do you care? I know the only reason you came to us is because you couldn't get money for your play anywhere else. And now all of a sudden you're getting—what's the word, Terence?—"scruples?" Just because we're Italians, because we're not college graduates, or because Mike uses incorrect grammar, all of a sudden you want to know if our money's clean?

TERENCE: Angie, please, believe me, it has nothing to do with your being Italians or your grammar or anything else. It's just that I've never done anything like this before. And a million dollars!—well, a million dollars, well, it's frightening.

ANGIE: You think small, Terry, that's one of your problems. You don't like to take chances with your life.

TERENCE: That may in fact be true.

ANGIE: Fine! Who needs this? Go find your money someplace else. You want clean money, borrow from the Church. Go ask Mother Teresa to invest! Go ask Cardinal O'Connor! Go ask Bishop Tutu!

TERENCE: Angie, listen, I'm sorry, I apologize. I deeply, deeply apologize. I'm very embarrassed.

ANGIE (*realizing she's gone too far and shown him a side of herself that's not very flattering*): No, it's my fault, I'm way out of line. I've got no right talking to you like that. Sometimes I fly off the handle. I'm sorry.

TERENCE: It's all right, really. I take it as a sign that you care.

ANGIE: I do care.

TERENCE: But you see, the fact of the matter is, money notwithstanding, I'm just wondering if my play is ready for Broadway. Or anywhere else.

ANGIE: But it was a big hit in Buffalo!

TERENCE: Buffalo! What the hell does anyone know about plays in Buffalo? The whole thing's ridiculous. What do I know about murder, for the love of God?

ANGIE: What does anybody know about murder?

TERENCE: Don't you understand? I thought I was breaking new ground. I thought I had new and valuable insights into the nature of death! Into the . . . the metaphysics of dying! I had the audacity to think I could imagine what it was like to kill someone! And I've never even been to a funeral—never mind a funeral, not even a wake until tonight! Your Uncle Frankie was the first corpse I ever saw face to face!

ANGIE: What's the difference? You wrote a play! Nobody expects you to kill somebody just so you can write a better play!

TERENCE: No, Angie, it's premature, it's inauspicious, it's ill advised. I'll take another look at it when I go back to the university, do some revisions, smooth out the rough spots. Then, in a year or two, we can all sit down again and see where we are. I'll explain to your dad why I feel it's advisable to be getting out before we all get in too far and . . .

ANGIE: You can't get out, Terence.

TERENCE *(terrified):* What do you mean I can't get out?

ANGIE: I mean I won't let you throw this opportunity away because you have this sudden irrational fear of . . . fear of success. There's nothing to be afraid of. Nothing can go wrong as long as I'm here.

TERENCE: But what if you're not here?

ANGIE: I'm not going anywhere.

TERENCE: You're not?

ANGIE: No. *(She kisses him)*

TERENCE: Angie, Angie! This isn't for me. It's really not for me. *(They kiss)* Maybe the murder's not so bad after all. Kiss me again.

ANGIE: Terence, it's like you said before. If you really believe is something, you don't get discouraged.

TERENCE *(kissing her):* I derive such strength from kissing you, such strength and optimism. *(They embrace passionately)*

ANGIE: I'm glad! *(Enter LOU)*

LOU: Hey! Hope I'm not interrupting anything.

ANGIE *(detaching herself from TERENCE):* No, we were just going over the eulogy Terry's writing. Where you been, over Frankie's house?

LOU: Yeah.

ANGIE: How's everybody?

LOU: You know. *(He goes behind the service bar and makes a drink)*

ANGIE: Whose idea was it, this creep Bertelli?

LOU: Uncle Mike got a good price, Bertelli owed him a favor. He's doing a nice job, don't worry about it.

ANGIE *(scornfully):* Nice, nice! That's not my idea of a nice job. *(TERENCE is startled by her tone of voice and looks at her)*

LOU: Don't worry about it.

ANGIE: Who's worried? I just don't like it, that's all. It doesn't look good. It looks cheap.

LOU: If it looks cheap, Mike's the one who looks cheap, not you and me. Anyway, I think he's doing a nice job.

ANGIE: Bertelli should be burying garbage, not people.

LOU: Your cousin Toni sends her love. I didn't know she was married.

ANGIE: Neither did I.

LOU: She looked good.

ANGIE: D'ja meet her husband?

LOU: He wasn't there. She looked very good. Got her teeth straightened out, looks like some work on her nose, lost some weight.

ANGIE: How much weight?

LOU: About fifty pounds. She asked me when *you* were getting married.

ANGIE: I'll get married when I get married.

LOU: Whataya think, Professor?

TERENCE: About what?

LOU: Don't you think it's about time Angel settled down?

TERENCE: Settled down? I'm about the last person in the world to have an opinion about your daughter's settling down!

ANGIE: Just lay off, Pop, okay? It's late, everybody's bushed.

TERENCE (*hazarding a clumsy pleasantry*): Anyway, I was under the impression that Italian fathers—I mean, ethnic parents—people who parent ethnically—I thought you didn't want your daughters to leave home.

LOU: Who's talking leaving home? We're talking marriage, we're not talking leaving home.

ANGIE: Yeah, well, we're *not* talking marriage. So let's knock it off as far as this subject is concerned.

LOU: What she wanna leave home for? She got everything her heart could desire, people waiting on her, hand and foot, right, hon?

TERENCE: No, yes, of course. I was thinking about her husband, that's all. Stupid.

LOU: What about her husband?

TERENCE: That her husband might have some ideas on the subject.

LOU: What subject?

TERENCE: Angie's leaving home. I thought her eventual husband might conceivably want to set up his own household somewhere else.

LOU: *Where* else?

TERENCE: Most married people—a lot of married people —some—do live separately from their parents or parents-in-law.

LOU: We're not good enough for her husband?

ANGIE: Honest to God! I'm gonna do the receipts. *(She exits)*

LOU: What's wrong with this character, he don't know a good deal when he sees it?

TERENCE: What character, Lou?

LOU: This husband of Angie's. What's *he* falling into like a bed of roses? I build them a house next door, three stories, four stories, Grandma lives upstairs, her sister lives downstairs, we have one rental for cash flow and liquid assets, how tough is this to take? They'll be happy living with me. What do they want I can't give them? Tell me what?

TERENCE: I don't know, I don't know what they want. Privacy maybe.

LOU: Who wants privacy? What is this privacy?

TERENCE: All I'm saying, maybe her husband will have some ideas about privacy.

LOU: He can learn to change his ideas, he can learn to adapt. Like you, take you, for instance.

TERENCE: What about me?

LOU: You can adapt, I seen you adapt, at Frankie's wake tonight you'd think you'd been doing wakes all your life.

TERENCE: That was an accident, I was drunk. I still am drunk, so you'll have to discount everything I say, which I'll deny tomorrow anyway when I sober up, *if* I sober up. But in general I have no flexibility whatsoever. I'm afraid I'm hopelessly stuck in my ways, creature of habit, unbudgeable actually.

LOU: I'm never wrong judging a man's character, and I ain't wrong about *you*, Terry.

TERENCE: You're wrong if you're thinking I'd ever give up my privacy to marry your daughter.

LOU: Hey, Terry, I don't know about marriage, but I come in you got your hands all over my daughter, you see what I mean, put yourself in my shoes, I can only assume your intentions are honorable, right under my nose, you follow me, Professor?

TERENCE: It wasn't what it looked like, Lou.

LOU: I didn't see what I saw, with your hands all over my kid?

TERENCE: Her hands were all over me, Lou, so help me, she was the aggressor.

LOU: But admit it, Terence, you weren't exactly repulsing her advances.

TERENCE: No, that's true, I wasn't, I'm sorry to say. I'm obviously in no condition to repulse anybody's advances.

LOU: Which where I come from amounts to encouraging the child.

TERENCE: The child? What child? I hope you're not referring to your daughter as a child, because if you are there are a few things about her you haven't really noticed, Lou.

LOU: Seems to me we're coming awful close to alienation of reflections.

TERENCE: Lou, Lou, I'm married. I'm already married. I'm a married man! And therefore I cannot under any circumstances be considered as a suitor for your daughter's hand in matrimony. I already have a hand in matrimony. My wife's hand. Her name is Sue Ellen, for the record—

LOU: The average marriage in this country lasts 5.2 years. I saw that in the *Reader's Digest.* How long you been married?

TERENCE: Thirteen years, seven months.

LOU: See what I mean? You're over the limit. Law of averages is catching up with you.

TERENCE: Lou, I'm too old for her!

LOU: Kind of man she needs, older fella, mature, man of the world. Give her security, give her kids.

TERENCE: I hate kids.

LOU: Nobody hates kids.

TERENCE: No, you're wrong, I do, I hate them with a passion. W.C. Fields was St. Francis of Assisi compared to me when it comes to kids.

LOU: You can learn to love them. Anyway her mind's made up.

TERENCE: *What?*

LOU: Her mind's made up and when Angie makes up her mind, that's it, it's finished. It's a foregone conclusion. 28 years I ain't won an argument with her and neither will you.

TERENCE: She told you she wants to marry me.

LOU: Easier to accept the inevitable.

TERENCE: She SAID that? In so many words?

LOU: She don't have to say it in so many words. I know what she's thinking. You're done for, pal.

TERENCE: I have to go home. I need some sleep, I need to sleep this off.

LOU: You can sleep at our house, Angie'll bring you.

TERENCE: No, Lou, I'm going to sleep in my own bed, in my own house.

LOU: You can't drive; you're too drunk to drive.

TERENCE: I can drive.

LOU: You'll kill yourself.

TERENCE: Good riddance.

LOU: Angie'll bring you, you can sleep on the couch in the living room, it's a Castro convertible, you'll love it.

TERENCE: No.

LOU: And in the morning, after the funeral, we'll talk about financing your play.

TERENCE *(as if he'd been struck in the face):* Financing my play?

LOU: I can tell you all the principals are very enthusiastic.

TERENCE: They are?

LOU: Believe me when I tell you. We'll discuss it tomorrow. Which one of these should we use in church?

TERENCE *(selecting one, rejecting it, selecting another):* This one . . . No, wait, that's such shit, such a pile of. . . . Here, this one, this one's not bad.

LOU *(reading):* "We come not to praise Frankie but to bury him." Great! I like that! *(Calling)* Angie! Let's go home!

ANGIE *(entering with an account book):* The tapes are off twenty-two ninety-five. You think she's ripping us off, this new kid?

LOU: Who? That Stacey?

ANGIE: Yeah, Stacey. There's something fishy about her.

LOU: Could be an honest mistake.

ANGIE: Let's get rid of her.

LOU: She's a nice kid.

ANGIE: I don't want her working for me!

LOU: What're we gonna tell her?

ANGIE: You're FIRED! How hard is that?

LOU: Do what you want, hon. It still seems to me like it could be an honest mistake.

ANGIE: She's gone.

LOU: It's up to you, you're the boss.

ANGIE *(kissing him):* Goodnight, Dad. See you tomorrow. What time's the funeral?

LOU: We should be at the church quarter to nine.

ANGIE: Bertelli comes drunk, tell him we'll burn his place down!

LOU: Lay off Bertelli, he's doing a nice job!

ANGIE: You tell him we'll burn him down. Call him and tell him.

LOU: 'Night, Professor. See ya in church! *(He leaves)*

TERENCE: You talk so . . . violently. "We'll burn the place down." Where does this come from?

ANGIE *(sweetly):* Oh, you have to talk to them in language they can understand if you want anything done the way it's supposed to be done. He knows I'm only joking.

TERENCE: Joking.

ANGIE: Of course. Come on. I'll drop you off.

TERENCE: Angie, I'm not going to attend this funeral.

ANGIE *(after reflection):* It won't look good.

TERENCE: I refuse to go to this funeral. There are limits.

ANGIE: You don't want to jeopardize the investment.
These guys are touchy, unpredictable, they have a lot
of Old World first generation values. I think you gotta
go.

TERENCE: Don't pressure me! Lay off! I'm tired of everybody pressuring me!

ANGIE: Who's pressuring you?

TERENCE: Nobody's gonna tell me what to do!

ANGIE: I'm only suggesting, I'm only advising you.

TERENCE: I don't need suggestions. I was pressured into
writing this eulogy, I was pressured into going to this
goddamned wake. Now you're pressuring me to go to
the funeral. Your father's pressuring me to marry you,
completely ignoring the fact that I'm already married—

ANGIE: Unhappily, by your own admission.

TERENCE: Be that as it may—

ANGIE: Nevertheless, nobody's pressuring you to do anything! Least of all to marry me, for Chrissake.
Where'd you get such an idea? It's unbelievable!

TERENCE: I agree.

ANGIE: What'd he say? What'd he say exactly?

TERENCE: I didn't take notes.

ANGIE: But still you must know.

TERENCE: Not verbatim.

ANGIE: You could make a summary.

TERENCE: It wasn't so much what he said but how he said it.

ANGIE: Just what I thought. He didn't say anything. You just imagined it. The whole thing's ridiculous. You're not even my type.

TERENCE: Oh? Is that right?

ANGIE: You're too old for me.

TERENCE (*injured vanity in spite of everything*): You said yourself we made a good-looking couple at the wake.

ANGIE: Wakes are not life! Besides, far be it from me to fling myself at someone who finds me unattractive.

TERENCE: I don't find you unattractive.

ANGIE: No, I suppose you find me desirable.

TERENCE: Heartbreaking!

ANGIE: Go home to your wife! Obviously you're still in love with her. Fine! Far be it from me to be a homewrecker.

TERENCE: Angie, I don't have a home to go home to. I don't have a wife, really. I haven't lived with her for five years. We're separated, we're getting a divorce. But the fact remains, I'm no kind of man for you. Look at me. What am I? I'm an empty shell, a husk, a nullity. A quarter of a century teaching English! They've squeezed me dry, there's nothing left, Angie. Whereas *you!* You're beautiful, beautiful and inspiring, a beautiful, young inspiring girl and I . . .

ANGIE: Inspiring? You find me inspiring? Really?

TERENCE: I haven't written a line of poetry since high school. But looking at you now, I could write Shakespeare's Sonnets for you. I could write *Paradise Lost* for you! I could write . . . Roget's *Thesaurus* for you!

ANGIE *(laughing):* You're drunk. You don't even know what you're saying. Come on, I'll drive you home.

TERENCE: I don't wanna go home.

ANGIE: Whataya gonna do? You can't stay here.

TERENCE: Your father said I could sleep on the Castro convertible in your living room.

ANGIE: He did? He said that?

TERENCE: That's what he said.

ANGIE: And is that what you really want to do?

TERENCE: Oh, yeah!

ANGIE: Then I have a better idea. There's also a Castro convertible back there in my office. In case you're wondering, only very slightly used.

(They kiss. Blackout)

Scene Three

It is evening of the following day. MIKE, LOU *and* TINO *are in the room.* MIKE *has a script of* TERENCE's *play in his hands.*

MIKE: The second act needs work.

LOU: *What?*

MIKE: In my opinion, the second act needs work. It don't seem real to me.

LOU *(scornfully):* Imagine, it don't seem real to him. Seems real enough to me. Seem real to you, Tino?

TINO: Real. What's "real"? What's real to me ain't necessarily real to you.

LOU: But what I'm asking is, *is* it real to you?

TINO: There's too much talk. Everybody's standing around talking!

LOU: That's what you do in a play. It ain't like television.

MIKE: That's all I'm saying. It ain't *real.*

LOU: So what the hell are we doing? We're sitting here and talking. Talk is real too.

MIKE: I don't like the title neither. You like the title, Tino?

TINO *(shrugging):* Hey, I buy and sell real estate. A title's a title.

LOU: What's wrong with the title?

MIKE: Look at all the great hits, they all had great titles. *Oklahoma! That* was a title. *The Student Prince.* See what I'm driving at? You hear it in your ears?

LOU: Where else I'm gonna hear it? In my nose?

MIKE: *The Student Prince.*

LOU: Fine, I'm sure Terry would have no objection to changing his title to *The Student Prince.* That's a great idea, I'm wondering why nobody else thought of it before.

MIKE: It's something to think about. *Pajama Games.* The great ones *all* had great titles. Name me one that didn't.

TINO: *Grease?*

LOU: Hey, we gonna back this show, or ain't we gonna back this show?

MIKE: Naturally we're gonna back this show. Our word is our word, ain't it? And we give him our Word of Honor, didn't we?

TINO: Not in so many words we didn't.

MIKE: What?

TINO: Give him our word.

MIKE: Lou, clear this up for me. Did we or did we not give him our word?

LOU: Like Tino says, not in so many words.

MIKE: I think we gotta be careful how we handle this character.

LOU: Why?

MIKE: Well, he's certainly a cold-blooded fucker.

LOU: Cold-blooded! Jesus Christ—

MIKE: Hey, dincha read the play? This description of ic-
ing this bird?

LOU: Hey, it's literature! Whataya think?

MIKE: You say it's literature. *I* say you don't make up
things like this out of your head.

LOU: Whataya trying to say, Mike? That Terry's a hit
man?

MIKE: I'm saying that some of these descriptions have
the ring of authenticity.

TINO: He was sleeping at the funeral. For what that's
worth.

MIKE: There! See? That's what I mean. What the hell
kind of character is this he falls asleep in the middle
of his own eulogy? Lemme ask you something, Louie.
What do we really know about him? Nutting, right?
Next to nutting.

LOU: Hey, what can I tell you? Angie's got a hard-on for
him.

TINO: Angie's got a hard-on for him? I had no idea.

MIKE: You sure?

LOU: Am I her father?

TINO: This is serious?

LOU: Very serious.

MIKE: I see. And you got no objection to your kid taking up with a goon?

LOU: He ain't no goon, he's a professor in the university!

MIKE: Could be a cover.

LOU: He's been there fifteen years.

MIKE: Could be a very deep cover.

TINO: Joey says the limited partnership papers are completely correct and legitimate.

MIKE: That makes me suspicious by itself.

LOU: Hey, what do we care? We take a plunge, what's the difference?

MIKE: That's easy for you to say, there's family involvement.

LOU: You worried about Angie?

MIKE: I like to think I can make up my own mind without having to be concerned with Angie's feelings.

LOU: Never mind about Angie's feelings. Family is family, business is business. Angie knows that.

MIKE: I'm glad to hear you say it, Louie. Because sometimes Angie can be headstrong, no criticism intended and take no offense.

LOU: She is headstrong. So what?

MIKE: Like I said, I don't mean to criticize.

LOU: You got nothing to complain about Angie. Who's got any complaints about Angie? You, Mike? Tino? Has Joey?

TINO: Nobody's complaining! You can analyze without your having to take everything so personal.

LOU: I ain't being personal! I give a shit!

TINO: Fine! I give a shit, too!

MIKE: Me also.

TINO: There. Everybody gives a shit equally.

LOU: Good.

MIKE: Fine.

TINO: Agreed.

MIKE *(after a long pause):* All the same, it just don't figure. What do *you* think, tell me the truth. You think it figures, this bird, Terence?

TINO: Yeah, I think it figures.

MIKE: Yeah? Okay, if you think so, okay.

TINO: Within limits I think it figures.

LOU: What limits?

TINO: You know, the limits just like Mike said, that we're dealing here with a murderous cold-blooded fucker. Outside of that I have no reservations whatsoever.

MIKE: Outside of that, me neither. Don't get me wrong, Louie. That's all I was saying. (*Enter* ANGIE *and* TERENCE)

LOU: Hey, doll, where ya been?

ANGIE: We went over Toni's for a drink. I thought you were telling me last night how great she looked, that she had her teeth straightened and everything.

LOU: She does look great, whatasa matter with you?

ANGIE: She looks like a cow.

MIKE: The eulogy was very good, Professor. Congratulations.

TERENCE: It went okay?

MIKE: Believe me when I tell you, there wasn't a dry eye in the joint.

TINO: I thought Eddie was good too.

LOU: Yeah, but Eddie ain't no Giulio.

TINO: What the hell's that mean, Eddie ain't no Giulio? Who's Giulio? Giulio's Giulio!

LOU: That's all I'm saying! Whataya getting so hot under the collar? Let's have a drink.

MIKE: Yeah, let's get this over with. I told Rose I'd be home early.

LOU *(to* ANGIE*)*: Whataya gonna have, doll?

ANGIE: No, nothing. I'll leave you guys alone to do your business. This doesn't concern me. *(She goes out.* LOU *brings a bottle and glasses from the service bar)*

MIKE *(as* LOU *pours drinks for everybody)*: So about your play, Professor . . .

TERENCE *(blurting it out)*: Yes, well! Now I realize that there's a very basic problem here with stretching the willing suspension of disbelief of any audience so far past the breaking point that . . . that . . . that it wouldn't even be funny. So I'm perfectly resigned to the idea that you don't feel very confident about sinking a lot of money into what is after all a really dubious project, me being a completely unknown playwright, and why have I even been wasting your valuable time, so . . . so let's just, why don't we just forget the whole thing! No hard feelings. Cheers! *(He empties his glass)* Cheers! *(He empties a second glass)*

MIKE: So what are you saying, Professor?

TERENCE *(Nervously, without realizing what he's doing, he grabs* MIKE's *glass and drains that too)*: Fuck it! Cheers!

LOU: Hey, Terry! What? You trying to tell us you've found other sources of revenue?

MIKE: The deal's off? Is that what I'm hearing, Lou?

TERENCE: The murder is ridiculous. Nobody's going to believe it for two seconds!

LOU: You're worried about people not believing the murder element?

TERENCE: I should be writing Noel Coward sex comedies. I should be writing flapdoodle for television! I should rewrite my thesis on Christina Rossetti!

TINO: I never knew Rossetti had a kid name of Christina!

TERENCE (*erupting with frustration*): IT'S A DIFFERENT ROSSETTI!

LOU: Well, you do what you want, Professor, but I'm going to tell you, the way we look at it, the murder is a little *too* believable. Naturally, what do we know?

TERENCE: You thought *what?* What did you say about the murder?

LOU: One of the criticisms we have is that the whole thing about the murder might be too strong.

TERENCE (*shocked, but quick to grasp the potential of the misunderstanding*): Oh yeah? You think it sounds authentic? Like . . . I know what I'm talking about?

CARL A. RUDISILL LIBRARY
LENOIR-RHYNE COLLEGE

TINO: It made my blood run cold.

TERENCE: Oh yeah?

MIKE: It's the work of a real professional.

TERENCE: It is? Is it, Mike? Well, God, coming from *you* that's a real compliment.

MIKE: Why coming from me?

TERENCE (*correcting hastily*): Why, because . . . well, because . . . because . . . obviously because you have such a *feel* for drama. Because you have such a sensitivity for theatre. That's all I meant.

MIKE: Some people might wonder where a college professor gets ideas like that.

TERENCE (*more and more emboldened to exploit their credulity*): Hey, well, you know, the university isn't exactly a sheltered workshop! We don't sit around in faculty meetings throwing intellectual puffballs at each other! It's a jungle out there. An eye for an eye, a tooth for a tooth.

LOU: I had no idea.

TERENCE: Most people don't. And it's probably a good thing too.

MIKE: But then what's all this song and dance? What happened overnight you come in here today and the deal's off?

TERENCE (*stalling, trying to think of something*): Well, you know . . . as far as I could see, the deal was never actually "on," was it?

TINO: You been talking to Sonny and Blow-Pipe Tubatini, by any chance?

TERENCE: Blow-Type Bubatini?

MIKE: Naturally he's been talking to Sonny and Blow-Pipe! What else? Why didn't I think of that? I wondered what they were doing hanging around the wake. I should of known! So. Blow-Pipe came to you with a better deal, right, Professor?

LOU: What kind of a deal can Blow-Pipe offer Terry?

MIKE: Blow-Pipe's suffering lately from—how do you call that, Tino?

TINO: Delusions of grandeur.

MIKE: Exactly the term I was looking for. He's booked a couple nightclub acts into his crummy casino down Atlantic City and now he thinks he's The Sound of Music! So, you're talking to Blow-Pipe, Terence. Blow-Pipe wants to produce your play.

TERENCE: Well, you know, Mike, people talk, right? Talk is cheap. You talk, you listen.

MIKE: Lemme tell you something, Terry. You don't mind I call you Terry? You remind me of my own son in some distant fashion. I can only speak for myself, but

I know I speak for all of us when I say that in our opinion your whole future is in front of you and we want to get behind you.

TERENCE: Well, that's good to hear, Mike. As a matter of fact, you remind me of my father—also in some distant fashion.

MIKE: Naturally you're free to shop this project around. We wouldn't dream of standing in your way. But lemme tell you something. Blow-Pipe Tubatini ain't exactly when it comes to the Roar of the Greasepaint and the Smell of the Crowd—Blow-Pipe ain't exactly . . . he ain't exactly . . .

TINO: He ain't exactly Daniel Merrick.

MIKE: That's all I'm trying to say.

TINO: So let's put our cards on the table, Professor. Whataya want, whataya need?

TERENCE *(taking a breath, taking a plunge):* Well, a non-returnable option payment of thirty-thousand dollars for six months. Seven percent royalty, no, *eight* percent royalty on the box office gross until recoupment and then ten, no, *twelve* percent thereafter. Script approval, cast approval, director and designers approval. *Plus:* I retain all movie, television and foreign language rights, though you can bid on these within three, no, *two* weeks of the closing performance. And my agent will call on your lawyers tomorrow to sign a letter of intent and the thirty-thousand dollar advance is payable immediately. *(There is a silence. The three friends look at each other)*

LOU: Sounds reasonable to me.

TERENCE: It does?

MIKE: Me too. You, Tino?

TINO: Hey, what do I know? Do what you want.

MIKE: Fine, then we got a deal—as long as you're willing to make some small changes in the script.

TERENCE: Changes? What kind of changes?

MIKE: Well, like Louie said before. The murder description seems too strong. And I think the title needs work.

TERENCE: The title?

LOU: Mike thinks you should change the title to *The Student Prince. (Enter* ANGIE)

ANGIE: How's it going?

TERENCE: We're into the creative side of the negotiations. Mike doesn't like the title.

ANGIE: What's wrong with the title, Uncle Mike?

MIKE: Ain't nothing *wrong* with it, Angie. I just thought it could use some work.

ANGIE: I love the title. You don't like the title, write your own play.

MIKE: Just a suggestion!

TERENCE: No, no! I mean, fair enough. I can take another look at the script, the title, the murder. There's always a certain amount of revision that goes on during rehearsals anyway—rewriting, adding, subtracting.

ANGIE: Oh yeah? I didn't realize this.

TERENCE: Oh sure. Nothing's written in stone.

ANGIE: Well, that's very interesting. Because, well, normally I wouldn't say anything, but as long as we're talking about revisions, and this is really not a criticism, it's just an observation, but the whole thing seems a little . . . it seems a little . . .

TINO: A little verbose!

ANGIE: Verbose, yeah! And like it all takes place in one room. I hate that.

TERENCE: But it has to take place in one room.

ANGIE: Why?

TERENCE: Well, because. It just has to! I'm not going to give you a lecture, Intro to Drama 101 . . .

ANGIE: Oh, I'm not trying to tell you what to do. I'm just saying that I personally don't like plays that take place in one room. And it is a little verbose.

TERENCE: Well, I suppose I can do some line-cutting.

MIKE: D'ja ever stop and think—as long as we're laying our cards on the table here what we don't like about this project—d'ja ever stop and think what if, and that's all I'm saying, understand. What if. Just think in those terms for a minute. What if. I'm not saying we should do this, but WHAT IF!

TERENCE: What if what?

MIKE: What if there was some music in this play?

TERENCE: Music? You want a musical about murder?

LOU: Certainly be something different, Terry.

TERENCE: You want musicals about murder, go to the Metropolitan Opera. They do one every night.

MIKE: The question that I see as I see it is what makes people feel good in this day and age?

TERENCE: I'm not interested in making people feel good!

MIKE: At fifty bucks a ticket, you want to make 'em feel bad?

TERENCE: We're not really talking about the same thing.

LOU: But Mike's got a point, Terry. Whatever else you can say in favor of murder, it don't make anyone feel good.

MIKE: Maybe this play shouldn't be about murder. Why can't it be about cats, for instance? Something people can hum the songs and tap their feet to the music.

TINO: I hate cats.

MIKE: It don't have to be cats. Dogs, then. Chimpanzees!

LOU: You can't have a musical about chimpanzees!

MIKE: Why not? It would be something different. People don't want to see the same old thing all the time. They want to see *Oklahoma!* They want to see *The Gypsies*.

TERENCE: Well, I'll certainly give it a great deal of thought.

MIKE: One other little thing. My wife, Rose, got this niece, cutest kid you ever saw. And talented? She's got more talent than you can shake a stick at. I was thinking maybe you could give her something in the play. Nothing major, you understand, just a small part, get her feet wet.

TERENCE: Your wife's *niece*?

MIKE: You name it, she can do it. Sing, tap dance, plays the accordion like nobody's business.

TERENCE: The accordion.

MIKE: I love accordion music. Don't tell me you don't like accordion music.

TERENCE: No, no, no! I'm wild about accordion music. It's just that in this play . . .

MIKE: Her name's Carmella. She was named after Carmen Cavallero, may he rest in peace, great piano player in his own right, friend of the family, probably before your time.

TERENCE: Look, Mike, I'd like to be . . . accommodating, naturally, but what you no doubt don't fully realize about professional theatre is that . . .

MIKE: It would make a world of difference. See, the kid's depressed. Fact of the matter is, she's got a weight problem and she thinks she's ugly. What do you call this psychological sickness? Embolism? Botulism?

TINO: She's fat.

MIKE: But a chance to do a part in a Broadway play would give her some confidence in herself.

TERENCE: I'm sorry to be blunt.

MIKE: I wouldn't have it any other way. Feel free.

TERENCE: I don't want to hurt your feelings.

MIKE: Go ahead. Say what's on your mind.

TERENCE *(passionately):* There's no part in this play for a fat teenage accordion player!

LOU: Careful what you say about Carmella, Terry. The kid's got feelings too, you know.

TERENCE: I'm sorry, but you see, I feel it's incumbent on me to . . .

TINO *(ominously):* You give a part to Carmella, you got to write a part for Filomena.

TERENCE: Who's Filomena?

TINO: *My* niece.

TERENCE: I suppose she plays the accordion too.

TINO: No, but she can learn.

LOU: I been thinking. You know where this show would go over great? In Uncle Luigi's restaurant in Tampa Bay. He's been talking for years about doing dinner theatre. He'll jump at the opportunity.

TERENCE: Wait a minute! Dinner theatre you do things like *Annie.* My play isn't remotely like *Annie.*

MIKE: What's wrong with *Annie? Annie* was a big hit, you should be so lucky.

TINO *(singing):* "Tomorrow . . . tomorrow . . ."

TERENCE: Wait a minute!

LOU: Hey, didn't Luigi's wife used to be an opera singer?

TERENCE: Wait a minute!

MIKE: We get Luigi interested in this scam, believe me, price is no object. Not that price is an object, but you get Luigi behind you, the sky's the limit!

TERENCE *(with a desperate scream):* WAIT A MINUTE! *(Silence. They all look at him innocently)* I'm sorry. Listen. I'm sorry, but you really don't understand. Revisions are one thing. Revisions are revisions. But what you're talking about are not revisions.

MIKE: These ain't revisions, Terry? What are they?

TERENCE: You're talking about changing fundamental concepts and I can't agree to that. I have to draw the line somewhere. There's an integrity to my play that can't be stretched beyond a certain point.

MIKE *(after a long pause):* I'm sorry to see your mind is completely closed to a little constructive criticism.

LOU: So am I. And to tell you the truth, Terry, I'm a little surprised.

MIKE: We're putting a million bucks into this piece of shit, Professor! Don't we get nutting for our money?

TERENCE: Okay, look! This just isn't going to work. Let's just forget the whole thing. It was crazy to think we could ever pull this off.

MIKE: What are you driving at, Professor?

TERENCE: It's probably hard for you to grasp this, Mike, but I didn't write this play to make money.

ANGIE: Terry, what are you saying?

TERENCE: I'll look for financing somewhere else.

ANGIE: Where else? There is nowhere else! You said yourself . . .

MIKE: He's been talking to the Tubatinis.

ANGIE: What? Uncle Blow-Pipe? They want to back his play?

LOU: That's what it sounds like, doll.

ANGIE: You can't let Blow-Pipe steal this play!

LOU: What're we gonna do? You heard him. He's not willing to make any compromises.

ANGIE: Do you realize that Julie just got divorced?

LOU: Julie? Julie who?

ANGIE: Julie Tubatini! Sonny's daughter! Are you crazy? You think I'm going to let that man-eating bitch get her hands on Terry?

LOU: Hey, doll! We're talking business, remember? This ain't exactly the place to—

ANGIE: We are talking the man I've been waiting for for twenty-eight years! That's what we're talking! You want me to get married? You want me to give you grandchildren?

LOU: Hey, watch your mouth!

ANGIE: I'm warning you, Pop—if he goes, I go!

LOU: Calm down, Angel, calm down. Don't be threatening your own father. Is this how I raised you?

ANGIE: Don't tell me to calm down, I am perfectly calm! And I'm telling you, either you produce Terry's play, or I swear to God, I'm leaving home!

LOU *(staggered):* You wouldn't!

ANGIE: Yes I would!

LOU: You couldn't!

ANGIE: Try me!

LOU *(appealing to the others):* Hey, what am I gonna do? You see how it is.

MIKE: It's not your fault, Louie. It's not entirely your fault. Okay, Professor. You got us over a barrel. You got a gun to our collective head. But at least give us a walk-on for my niece.

TERENCE: No, I'm sorry, it's not possible. No relatives. No Uncle Luigi. No Uncle Luigi's wife!

MIKE: Then at least how about a little background music, to set the mood.

TERENCE: I don't think so.

MIKE: Before the show. In the lobby. While the people are coming in. A little Perry Como, a little Jerry Vale. A little Lou Monte. How about it, Professor. Throw us a bone.

TERENCE: Well, maybe a little Pavarotti.

ANGIE: No, I think that's a bad idea. Absolutely not! No music! You do the play exactly the way Terence wrote it, word for word, take it or leave it. (TINO, LOU *and* MIKE *look at each other helplessly*)

TERENCE: Well, gentlemen, do we have a deal or don't we? *(The three partners huddle briefly, confer, decide)*

MIKE: We got a deal. (ANGIE *and* TERENCE *embrace.* MIKE *turns on* LOU) Next time raise your kid right!

LOU: Mike, just think of it. Opening night . . . Connie Chung, Channel 5 News, Pavarotti, Lou Monte, some bimbo under our arms! (MIKE *laughs*)

ANGIE: Let's have a drink to celebrate the partnership. *(She brings glasses of champagne for everyone)*

LOU *(passing out glasses):* Mike, Tino . . . have a drink.

TERENCE *(toasting):* Mike, Lou, Tino . . . Break your legs! *(As they all drink, the lights black out. End of play)*

"The fun comes gift-wrapped."
—CLIVE BARNES,
New York Post

BREAKING LEGS BY TOM DU LACK

Getting your play produced these days requires luck under the best of circumstances, but when the pinstripes in your angels' suits are as wide as the proscenium, "break a leg" takes on a whole new meaning.

A doting father, Lou Graziano is anxious to give his daughter Angie anything her heart desires. Angie lusts after her college English professor, on sabbatical shopping his new play around. Graziano's associate Mike Francisco sees an opportunity to go legit and magnanimously offers to give the fellow whatever he needs to put up a first-class production. Only Mike would like to discuss some changes: a new title, some music maybe, a part for his wife's overweight niece, the accordion player.... The chance of a lifetime is dangling in front of Terence O'Keefe...can he grab it before it grabs him?